STECK-VAUGHN

W9-CHH-789

transitions
preparing
for
college
writing

Carol Jago

Steck
Vaughn®

HOUGHTON MIFFLIN HARCOURT

www.SteckVaughn.com/AdultEd
800-289-4490

Photo Acknowledgements: Page cover ©L. Clarke/Corbis; 7 ©rubberball/Getty Images; 45 ©Jeffrey Coolidge/Photodisc/Getty Images; 89 ©moodboard/Corbis; 131 ©Alloy Photography/Veer; 171 ©Dougal Waters/Digital Vision/Getty Images.

Printed in the United States of America

ISBN 13: 978-1-419-07474-5
ISBN 10: 1-419-07474-1

2 3 4 5 6 7 8 9 0956 17 16 15 14 13 12 11 10

Contents

Using this Book

The *Transitions: Preparing for College* series moves adult learners successfully into a college classroom without having to spend valuable time or money on remedial, not-for-credit courses. Specifically written with adult learners in mind, this two-book series provides learners with the skills necessary for mastering college entrance exams and college coursework.

In the *Transitions: Preparing for College Writing* book, each unit leads students through the writing process, including prewriting, drafting, revising, editing, and examining model essays, ultimately guiding students to create polished, authentic essays. The five most common types of college writing are highlighted: persuasive, expository, reflective, literary analysis, and writing in response to a prompt. Writing, grammar, and mechanics instruction are woven seamlessly into the individual steps of the writing process, giving learners a chance to master these skills in the context of their own writing.

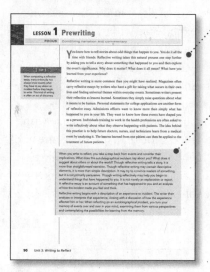

Informal Introduction

Each lesson begins with an introduction of the target concept using language and contexts that adult learners will understand and connect with, including real-world applications and examples.

Formalization

The formalization box follows the introduction. The actual "teaching" part of the lesson, this section presents the lesson's target academic skill in bite-sized chunks that allow students to master concepts gradually.

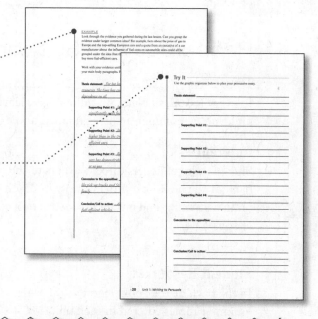

Example

After the formalization of the target skill, learners are shown how to apply the concept in carefully scaffolded, guided examples. Answers are provided so that learners can assess their own understanding of the material.

Try It

This section challenges learners to apply their knowledge to independent practice or their own writing. Each lesson leads learners through the next step in the writing process, ultimately enabling learners to internalize the writing, grammar, and mechanics instruction and incorporate it into their gradually evolving, authentic essay.

Know It!

Each lesson ends with a *Know It!*, which sums up the lesson, reminding learners what is the most important kernel of knowledge they should take away.

KNOW IT! When writing an expository essay, you will often need to paraphrase and summarize information. Remember, a summary is always shorter than the original, while a paraphrase can be as long as or longer than the original. A summary focuses only on main ideas and the most important details, while a paraphrase includes all of the details, big and small. Both summaries and paraphrases are written in your own words. Even though the information is expressed in your own words, you must still give credit to your sources. Keep notes of where you found information and cite your sources.

Self-Assessment

Are You Ready to Go On?

This feature appears at natural checkpoints in the writing process, prompting learners to assess their progress to determine if they should continue with the lessons—and move to the next step in the writing process—or go back and work a little more before moving on.

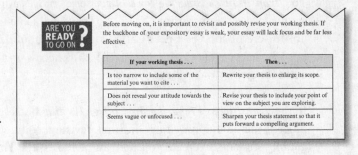

Wrap It Up

At the end of each unit, learners spend time assessing their final draft and reflecting on their unique experience with the writing process. Learners first self-assess their polished essay using a genre-specific rubric that was originally introduced earlier in the unit. They then complete a guided self-reflection, focusing on their experience with the writing process for that specific genre and noting the highlights, lowlights, and things they want to remember for the next time they must create that type of essay.

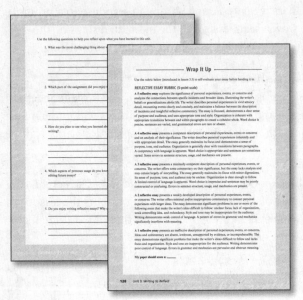

Resources and Support

Tips

In every lesson, side-margin callouts give learners general tips, hints, notes, common errors, guidance, and extra support.

References

Side-margin references direct learners to the resources in the back of the book that provide more in-depth information on the grammar and mechanics instruction covered in the lessons.

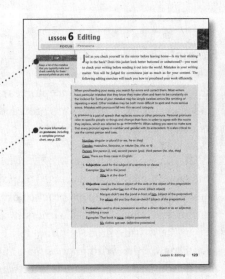

Student Resources

In the back of the book, learners are provided with a *Grammar Handbook* that expands on the grammar topics covered in each unit, *MLA Guidelines*, a chart of *Common Editing Marks*, a *Glossary*, and an *Index*. Learners can also access *Student Tips for Success*, which provides survival tips for making the most of campus resources as well as time management tips and college best practices to make their collegiate experience a successful one.

UNIT **1** Writing to Persuade

LESSON 1 Prewriting

Y ou have had practice with the art of persuasion since you were a child. Seven-year-olds can make remarkably convincing arguments when persuading their parents to get a dog or buy candy in the grocery store checkout line. They know they must address parental objections and offer evidence of their own competence in animal care or with a toothbrush. This unit will help you to refine your persuasive skills and, in the process, teach you how to produce a college-level persuasive essay.

When you write to **persuade**, your goal is to convince your audience to agree with you. You attempt, with your **essay**, to influence a reader's **point of view** and actions. To do this, you will need to:

1. convince the reader of your sincerity as well as your expertise and knowledge about the issue.

2. offer the reader clear and logical reasons for thinking as you do.

3. appeal to the reader's emotions through compelling examples and careful word choice.

EXAMPLE

The best way to learn how to write effective persuasive essays is to examine how others attempt to persuade. This will help you discover the tools of persuasive **argument**. Let's examine one of the most famous speeches in American history, Abraham Lincoln's Gettysburg Address. The speech was delivered on November 19, 1863 on the battlefield near Gettysburg, Pennsylvania.

"Fourscore and seven years ago our fathers brought forth on this continent a new nation, conceived in liberty, and dedicated to the proposition that all men are created equal.

Now we are engaged in a great civil war, testing whether that nation, or any nation so conceived and so dedicated, can long endure. We are met on a great battlefield of that war. We have come to dedicate a portion of that field as a final resting-place for those who here gave their lives that this nation might live. It is altogether fitting and proper that we should do this.

But, in a larger sense, we cannot dedicate . . . we cannot consecrate . . . we cannot hallow . . . this ground. The brave men, living and dead who struggled here, have consecrated it far above our poor power to add or detract. The world will little note nor long remember what we say here, but it can never forget what they did here. It is for us, the living, rather, to be dedicated here to the unfinished work which they who fought here have thus far so nobly advanced. It is rather for us to be here dedicated to the great task remaining before us . . . that from these honored dead we take increased devotion to that cause for which they gave the last full measure of devotion; that we here highly resolve that these dead shall not have died in vain; that this nation, under God, shall have a new birth of freedom; and that government of the people, by the people, for the people, shall not perish from the earth."

Notice how Abraham Lincoln uses carefully chosen words to communicate important ideas about war and about the sacrifices that brave men have made to preserve the union. He made his listeners—and contemporary readers—feel how important the men's contribution was. Reread the speech and underline all the words and phrases that you think create an emotional response from a listener or reader.

1. How do words like *consecrate, hallow,* and *nobly* make you feel about the men who died on the battlefield?

_____

_____

_____

_____

_____

_____

2. How does Lincoln's choice of words reveal how he wants his listeners to react? What is he trying to persuade his listeners to believe or do?

_____

_____

_____

_____

_____

3. How do Lincoln's references to "unfinished work," "great task," "died in vain" appeal to his listeners' better selves and contribute to his persuasive argument?

_____

_____

_____

_____

_____

■ Try It

Think of an issue you care deeply about. If you have trouble coming up with an idea, pick up a newspaper or scan an online news site for current topics. You could also watch the nightly news on television for ideas.

Write freely for five minutes about this issue. Give full expression to your strong feelings and convictions on the topic.

_____

_____

_____

_____

_____

_____

_____

_____

_____

_____

Now that you have your initial response down on paper, try to write a clear and coherent sentence or pair of sentences that express your opinion about the topic. This is your **thesis**. Your thesis has two goals: it should make readers aware of the issue you will be discussing and it should tell readers how you feel about it.

An example of a thesis statement calling for cars with better gas mileage might read: "For too long American cars have guzzled up American resources. The time has come for carmakers and car owners to overcome their dependence on oil." Notice how this thesis identifies the topic (the overconsumption of American resources—namely oil—by American car drivers) and the author's opinion about the topic (carmakers and owners need to change their behavior).

Draft a **working thesis statement** on the lines below.

_____

_____

_____

_____

Read your thesis statement to see if it seems clear and coherent. Ask yourself or a friend:

Does my thesis state the issue clearly?	**If not,** identify more precisely the issue you are writing about.	**If so,** proceed to the next question.
Does my thesis convey how I feel about the issue?	**If not,** identify more precisely where you stand on this issue.	**If so,** proceed to the next question.
Is my thesis clearly phrased?	**If not,** think how the issue could be rephrased for greater **clarity**.	**If so,** proceed to the next question.
Should I state the problem <u>more</u> dramatically?	**If so,** consider how to increase the sense of urgency.	**If not,** proceed to the next question.
Should I state the problem <u>less</u> dramatically?	**If so,** adopt a calmer tone.	**If not,** proceed to the next question.
Is my choice of words persuasive?	**If not,** replace weak word choices with more vivid, concrete words.	**If so,** you have written a coherent thesis statement!

After answering these questions, adjust and rewrite your thesis statement. The success of your persuasive essay will depend heavily upon your careful construction of this key statement.

Revised thesis statement:

_____

_____

_____

_____

_____

_____

[TIP]

The use of "I"
Phrases such as "I think" or "I believe" often creep into a thesis statement. Given that your persuasive essay is a statement of what you think and believe, using phrases like "I think" and "I believe" is unnecessary and detracts from the power of your argument. Eliminate them from your thesis statement. You will notice that this deletion will strengthen and streamline your thesis.

KNOW IT! While it is important to develop a thesis statement before you begin writing your essay, it may not end up being the first sentence of your paper. Often writers choose to open with an **anecdote** or statement of startling facts to grab a reader's attention. In other cases, writers of persuasive essays save their thesis for the concluding paragraph, subtly drawing readers along as they build up evidence and hitting them with a solution at the very end.

LESSON 2 Gathering Evidence

With your thesis statement written, it is time to ask yourself what else you need to know about this issue in order to develop your ideas into a persuasive essay. Think of questions you have about your subject and places where you might find answers to these questions. While researching your topic, be sure to consider the **credibility** of your **sources**.

- Does the individual whose work you are reading have demonstrated expertise in this area?

- Do the facts and numerical data that are cited come from a reliable source?

- Is the Web site you are visiting a credible source of information?

As you conduct your **research**, record information and **quotations** that could be used to support your thesis. Remember to include the speaker or author's name, the source, page number, and date of the publication in your notes. For Web sites copy the entire URL (Web site address). You must be careful not to represent someone else's ideas or words as your own. Keeping track of sources as you read will help you cite your **references** accurately.

In the course of your research you may discover **evidence** that supports an opposing point of view. Keep notes on this information as well. Addressing and refuting **counter-arguments** will strengthen your persuasive essay.

Use the following guidelines to help you determine the credibility of the information you find on Web sites:

- If a person's name appears as a source of information, ask yourself, "Who is this person? What is his or her background? Does this person have the expertise to be trusted?"

- Check the last three letters of the Internet address. Web sites that end in .edu originate from a college or university. The .gov suffix indicates a government agency. Both of these types of Web sites require oversight of their content and can usually be trusted. But beware! Some sites that end in .edu have been posted by students at a university or college and cannot be relied on without further confirmation of their content from other, more reliable sources.

- Pay attention to the purpose of the Web site. Try to determine if the sponsors of the site are advocating a particular position or hoping to sell a product.

- Confirm any information you cite from Wikipedia with other credible sources of information.

You have decided that it is important to increase the fuel efficiency of American automobiles. To gather evidence supporting your point of view, you begin to research information for an essay to persuade carmakers to increase fuel efficiency. When you come across an interesting piece of information or a fact that supports your thesis, write it down and record the source from where the information came.

Notes/Quotation: _"Cars in Japan get significantly better mileage than U.S. cars both in the cities and on the highways."_

Source: _Don Brinker, May 23, 2008, www.fuelefficiencyfacts.com_

Try It

Find evidence—quotations, statistics, and facts—to support the argument expressed in your thesis statement.

Note/Quotation: _____

_____

_____

_____

_____

_____

_____

Source: _____

_____

_____

Note/Quotation: _____

_____

_____

_____

_____

Source: _____

_____

_____

Note/Quotation: _____

_____

_____

_____

_____

_____

_____

_____

_____

_____

[TIP]

Remember that you must evaluate the credibility of all the sources you use. Few things can do more damage to the power of your argument than citing unreliable data or questionable sources.

Source: _____

_____

_____

Note/Quotation: _____

_____

_____

_____

_____

_____

_____

_____

_____

Source: _____

_____

_____

Note/Quotation: _____

_____

_____

_____

_____

_____

_____

_____

_____

Source: _____

_____

_____

[TIP]

The more fully you research your issue, the more likely you will be to write a compelling persuasive essay. While you may not change a reader's mind immediately, your argument should invite a reader to reconsider his or her position. You want a reader to pause and think, "Hmm . . . I never thought of it this way."

Note/Quotation: _____

_____

_____

_____

_____

_____

_____

_____

_____

_____

Source: _____

_____

_____

Incorporating Evidence

Incorporating research into your persuasive essay involves more than simply copying information you found into a **draft**. Sometimes you will want to use direct quotations. Other times you may choose to paraphrase what an expert has written. Whenever you cite evidence from another source, be sure to add commentary or analysis explaining *how* this information strengthens your argument. Don't take it for granted that a reader will see what you have seen in the evidence. You should always present supporting evidence within the context of your own argument, explaining clearly how it relates to your thesis.

Use the following sentence templates to help you fully incorporate and explain the importance and relevance of the information you collected in the course of your research. (Note: "This point" refers to the main idea of your paragraph.)

This point was demonstrated by _____

when he explained that, "_____

_____

_____

_____

_____ "

Additional evidence in support of this point can be found in _____

which shows _____

_____

_____ .

_____ offers another perspective on this issue when she argues that

_____

_____

_____ .

To **refute** evidence that runs counter to your argument, you might write:

While _____ claims that _____

_____

_____ , it can also be argued that _____

_____

_____

_____

Another way to refute evidence is to write:

Though I continue to insist that _____

_____ , individuals such as _____

contend that _____

_____ .

After working through the lesson on gathering evidence, you may find you have lost interest in the issue you initially chose for your essay. *Don't panic*. It's not too late to start over. Trying to persuade a reader on an issue you are bored with only makes the task more difficult.

If you are looking for a new subject, consider taking a pro or con position on one of these issues. It is also possible to write an effective essay that takes a middle ground, arguing both "Yes" and "No."

- Does violence in the media promote violence on the streets?
- Should junk mail be outlawed?
- Is it important to save endangered species?
- Should research scientists be allowed to experiment with animals?
- Is skateboarding a crime?
- Is plastic surgery a sign of a vain society?
- Do zoos respect the rights of animals?
- Should junk food and carbonated beverages be banned in schools?
- Should gifted high school athletes go pro?
- Is health care a human right?
- Is airport security making America safer?

LESSON **3** Drafting

The blank page can be terrifying. For many writers getting started is the hardest part of writing. Don't worry about having a perfect first sentence. You can add an engaging opening later. Right now your goal is to put a draft of your main ideas down on paper. Start with your thesis statement. Then present and analyze the evidence you have gathered to build your persuasive argument.

You may remember being taught in middle or high school to write a five-paragraph essay with an **introduction**, three **supporting points**, and a **conclusion**. Such structures help to organize your argument, but there is no hard and fast rule about how many paragraphs should be in a persuasive essay. Sometimes two strong supporting paragraphs are enough to make your argument. Other times you may find you have four or more supporting points to make. Consider the order in which you plan to present your supporting evidence, as well. Many writers save their strongest point for last. Others choose to present their most dramatic point first. The choice is up to you, but make sure that you present your evidence in a manner that makes your argument most powerfully. Allow what you have to say to determine the **organization** of your essay.

Somewhere in your persuasive essay you will need to address how a reader might disagree with you. This is called a **concession**. When you concede to the opposition, you present what the "other side" says about the issue and acknowledge the legitimacy of their point. You may choose to leave it at that, or you may choose to then discuss why your solution or position adequately addresses their position. Addressing counter-arguments is an important feature of effective **persuasive writing**. You may choose to make concessions to the opposition early in your draft or wait until you have made your points to address counter-arguments. Wherever you decide to address them, remember that addressing these concerns allows readers see that you have considered your issue carefully.

Many persuasive essays end with a **call to action** in which the writer tells readers what needs to be done in order to remedy the problem.

Look through the evidence you gathered during the last lesson. Can you group the evidence under larger common ideas? For example, facts about the price of gas in Europe and the top-selling European cars and a quote from an executive of a car manufacturer about the influence of fuel costs on automobile sales could all be grouped under the idea that the high cost of fuel in Europe motivates people to buy more fuel-efficient cars.

Work with your evidence until you have two, three, or four main points. These will be your main **body** paragraphs. For example:

Thesis statement: *For too long American cars have guzzled up American resources. The time has come for carmakers and car owners to overcome their dependence on oil.*

> **Supporting Point #1:** *Japanese carmakers have designed vehicles that are significantly more fuel efficient than American cars.*

> **Supporting Point #2:** *In Europe, where the price of gas is two to four times higher than in the United States, people drive much smaller, more fuel-efficient cars.*

> **Supporting Point #3:** *Research and development of hybrid and electric cars has demonstrated that it is possible to design cars that use less or no gas.*

Concession to the opposition: *Some people need to operate gas-guzzling vehicles like pick-up trucks and SUVs either for their work or to transport a large family.*

Conclusion/Call to action: *Americans must drive less and begin to use more fuel-efficient vehicles.*

■ Try It

Use the graphic organizer below to plan your persuasive essay.

Thesis statement: _____

_____

_____

_____

Supporting Point #1: _____

_____

_____

Supporting Point #2: _____

_____

_____

Supporting Point #3: _____

_____

_____

Supporting Point #4: _____

_____

_____

Concession to the opposition: _____

_____

_____

_____

Conclusion/Call to action: _____

_____

_____

_____

Developing Your Supporting Paragraphs

Now that you have the bare bones of your essay down on paper, it is time to develop each of your supporting points into supporting paragraphs. You can do this in several different ways. The most effective essays use a combination of the following techniques:

1. Offer an anecdote as an example from your own experience. On the lines below briefly retell a story about something that happened to you or to someone you know that illustrates the point you want to make.

_____

_____

_____

_____

_____

_____

_____

_____

_____

2. Analyze every quotation you cite. On the lines below copy one quotation from your research and then offer commentary on how this quote supports your argument. Don't assume that your readers will automatically see why it is relevant.

Quotation: _____

_____

_____

How does this quotation support the point you are making? Comment on its significance to your argument.

_____

_____

_____

_____

_____

_____

3. Explain how any data, research, or statistics contribute to your argument. Simply providing evidence isn't enough. You need to connect it to your thesis, explaining to your audience how the numbers strengthen your argument.

Data or piece of evidence: _____

_____

_____

How does this evidence support your thesis?_____

_____

_____

_____

_____

_____

Repeat this process for every main supporting point in your paper.

Appeals to Logic and Emotion

Every day you are bombarded by persuasive texts in the form of advertising. The purpose of advertising is to persuade consumers to purchase particular products or services. Effective ads appeal both to buyers' logic *and* emotions. For example, automobile ads commonly cite the performance of their vehicles in an accident as well as the vehicle's fuel efficiency and low-maintenance qualities. These aspects of the ad appeal to a buyer's desire for safety and economy. Automobile ads also often include attractive young men and women driving their cars to fancy restaurants or exotic, far-away places. These aspects of the ad appeal to a buyer's emotions and desires.

As you construct your persuasive argument, consider how you might appeal to readers' logic and emotions. Writers appeal to logic by citing hard evidence in the form of data, expert testimony, or research. Writers appeal to emotion through the use of dramatic word choice, vivid images, and shocking examples. Use the graphic organizer below to help you incorporate appeals to logic and emotion in one of your supporting points.

Supporting Point: _____

_____

_____

_____

_____

_____

APPEALS TO LOGIC (facts, data, expert testimony, etc.)	APPEALS TO EMOTION (examples and descriptions that appeal to readers' desires, fears, sympathy, or other feelings)

Repeat this process for every main supporting point in your paper. The best arguments will have an effective combination of logical and emotional appeals throughout.

Time to Write

Draft your persuasive essay on the following pages. Don't worry if you find yourself writing about things that didn't appear in your graphic organizers. New points will come to you as you compose. Let the act of writing help your ideas evolve.

[TIP]

Try to work on this draft in a place where you won't be distracted or interrupted. You need be able to concentrate.

_____

_____

_____

_____

_____

_____

_____

_____

_____

_____

_____

_____

_____

_____

_____

_____

_____

_____

_____

KNOW IT!

A counter-argument is an argument in opposition to the case you are making. There can often be more than one counter-argument. Considering these can help you make your case more completely.

A concession to the opposition is an admission of the legitimacy or value of a counter-argument. Acknowledging arguments from an opposing point of view helps your argument sound more reasonable and well thought out. It also provides you with an opportunity to highlight the importance of your own arguments.

You may find after drafting your essay that you need more information and need to do additional research. Identify points in your draft that you know are weak and spend some time finding evidence to strengthen them.

Before you begin revising your draft, let's take a look at a model of persuasive writing. One way to learn how to write an effective persuasive essay is to analyze how other writers craft written arguments. The following persuasive essay was written as a continuing feature about college readiness for a national soccer magazine. Pay attention to the ways in which the writer develops her persuasive argument.

Persuasive writing is central to journalism. Every newspaper in the country features opinion pieces in which writers express their views and try to persuade readers to agree. Whether the subject is politics, entertainment, business, or sports, columnists use the same persuasive tools you will use in your own writing for college: a thesis statement, supporting evidence, concessions to the opposition, and a conclusion that often includes a call to action.

Though the building blocks are similar, newspaper columns typically employ short paragraphs to facilitate quick reading. They are also written with the assumption that many readers will only scan the first few paragraphs. For this reason, journalists commonly state the point of view they want readers to adopt early in their columns—in the essay you are about to read, the thesis is stated in the headline—and lead with their strongest evidence first.

A journalist's evidence often consists of quotations from experts in the field whom the writer has interviewed, presented in a manner that strengthens the argument. You may decide that your persuasive essay could benefit from such supporting evidence.

EXAMPLE

Read the following article and ask yourself:

1. What is the writer attempting to persuade you of concerning preparation for college?

2. What evidence does the writer offer to support her claim?

3. How does the writer draw you in and make you care about the issue?

Thinking Matters

Preparing for college isn't just about scrutinizing college catalogues or taking entrance exams. It involves developing academic habits of mind. While having the stamina to read dense texts and write extended research papers is important, the most vital skill young people in pursuit of a college education need to possess is the ability to think.

When faculty from California's community colleges, state university system, and the University of California published a statement of competencies for entering students, I was immediately suspicious that this would be one more study from the ivory towers telling me what I as a high school teacher was doing wrong. It was nothing of the kind. The document describes the foundational dispositions well-prepared students have for academic reading, writing, and critical thinking. I cannot imagine any college in the country would disagree with their findings.

College faculty expect students to:

- have an appetite to experiment with new ideas, challenge their own beliefs, seek out other points of view, and contribute to intellectual discussions.
- apply analytical abilities to their own endeavors as well as to the work of others.
- generate critical responses to what they read, see, and hear, and develop a healthy skepticism toward their world.
- assume a measure of responsibility for their own learning.

Professors reported that while students are more diligent than in the past, many seem unwilling to engage in the hard work of thinking or analyzing unless it is directed to their immediate interests. Forty percent of the professors interviewed for this study said that their students' ability to tackle complex, analytical work has declined over the course of their teaching years. One commented that students' thought processes seem shallow, like sound bites.

In our effort to ensure that children have the basic skills they need to be academically competitive, we may have shortchanged the most basic skill of all—thinking. It is too easy to assign blame to popular culture and news programs. Their penchant for sound bites is duly recorded and deplored. They encourage a superficial analysis of issues. What we need to examine are the kinds of conversations occurring in classrooms. Do young people see models of intellectual discourse? Do they participate? Are they taken to task for faulty reasoning or shabby evidence? Have they experienced the pleasurable give and take of academic argument? I fear that such classroom discussions are all too rare.

The most common cause of poor writing is weak thinking. If a student cannot marshal the evidence to support a point of view in his head, he will find it difficult to do so on paper. University professors rarely walk students through a writing process to help them construct their essays. Papers are assigned. Entering college students are expected to be able to:

- analyze the ideas or arguments of others critically.
- summarize ideas or information contained in a text.
- synthesize ideas from several sources.
- report facts or narrate events.

For most of these assignments, students need to be able to generate an effective thesis; develop this thesis convincingly with well-chosen examples, good reasons, and logical arguments; and structure their writing so that it moves beyond formulaic patterns.

I fully understand teenagers' reluctance to think. Why bother thinking if someone else is willing to do the thinking for you? I'll tell you why. Because it means that someone else now has all the power. If my tenth grade students put half the energy they invest in planning Saturday night into literary analysis, their essays would improve dramatically. We need to help kids see that such an investment pays enormous dividends. Thinking matters. We must help our children do it more often.

1. What is the writer attempting to persuade you of concerning preparation for college?

    _____

    _____

    _____

    _____

    _____

    _____

    _____

2. What evidence does the writer offer to support her claim?

    _____

    _____

    _____

    _____

    _____

    _____

    _____

3. How does the writer draw you in and make you care about the issue?

    _____

    _____

    _____

    _____

    _____

    _____

    _____

Try It

Now that you have read through the essay once, reread it, paying attention to *how* the author accomplishes her purpose. Imagine the article is laid out before you on a laboratory table for dissection. Pick up your dissection tool (any pen or pencil will do) and:

1. Underline the thesis statement. Where in the article does the author state what she is attempting to persuade readers to think and believe? Is the thesis restated toward the end of the piece? Underline this sentence as well.

2. Circle words or phrases that the writer assumes readers of the article will understand without explanation (for example, SAT, ACT, ivory towers).

3. Draw a wavy line under stylistic techniques that draw the reader into the argument (for example, rhetorical questions like "Why bother thinking if someone else is willing to do the thinking for you?"). What effect do these techniques have on you, the reader?

4. Use two different colors to identify appeals to both logic and emotion within the essay. Notice how both are used to create a balanced persuasive approach.

5. Identify important supporting evidence in the article. List below the examples used to defend the essay's thesis.

* _____

  _____

  _____

* _____

  _____

  _____

* _____

  _____

  _____

* _____

  _____

  _____

* _____

  _____

  _____

[TIP]

Extend Your Learning
Choose an opinion piece on a topic you care about from today's newspaper or an online source and analyze it as you have "Thinking Matters." The Web pages for the following newspapers are excellent sources of model persuasive writing.

- *USA Today*
- *Houston Chronicle*
- *The Washington Post*
- *The Chicago Tribune*
- *The New York Times*
- *The Denver Post*
- *The Tennessean*

KNOW IT! Analyzing model essays is one way to learn what the best persuasive practices are and to see them in effect. Dissecting a model essay—analyzing where and how the thesis is stated and how the writer develops his or her argument through the use of supporting **details**, stylistic techniques, appeals to logic and emotion, and concessions to the opposition—will help you internalize these techniques, making it easier for you to use them in your own writing.

Think about the tools and techniques that professional writers use to persuade readers. What made the persuasive essays you just read so effective? What stylistic elements or persuasive techniques did you notice that you could use as you revise your own essay to make it more compelling and persuasive?

_____

_____

_____

_____

_____

_____

_____

_____

_____

_____

_____

_____

_____

_____

_____

_____

_____

_____

_____

_____

_____

_____

LESSON 5 Revising

When told to **revise**, students often mistakenly feel that the teacher is saying their essays are inadequate and that they are no good at writing. Not true! The teacher is more likely trying to demonstrate that the ideas in the paper are so good that they deserve more attention and polish. Asking you to revise is another way of telling you that your draft shows promise. All your essay needs is a bit more work to make it shine.

One way to make your essay shine is to write with **voice**. The voice you choose to use will depend upon your **audience**. Just as you would speak in a different style when talking with your friends, your boss, your family, or someone you just met, you should employ a different tone and voice when writing for different audiences.

As you sit down to revise your draft, keep your persuasive **purpose** at the forefront of your mind. The goal of your paper is to convince readers to think and feel as you do. An important first step is to consider the audience for your essay. The audience is made up of the intended readers of your paper. Do you think your readers already care about the issue, or are you attempting to persuade readers to consider an issue they have overlooked? Are you trying to open your readers' eyes to a point of view they have previously ruled out? Will your readers need to be provided with background information about your issue in order to be persuaded?

Assessing the nature of your audience will help you to determine the appropriate voice and **tone** for your essay. Voice refers to the **style** of your writing. It influences your choice of words and your **sentence structure**. It can be formal, informal, serious, humorous, concerned, insistent, or any other style you might use when talking to someone about something important to you. Your writing should sound like you!

Tone reflects your attitude and approach towards your subject. Do you want your audience to laugh with you at the folly of those who think differently? Do you want them to be impressed by your evidence and statistics? Do you want to convey your own learning on the subject? Your answers will help you to revise your draft and help it to achieve its purpose—to persuade others of your point of view.

Let's take a look at four statements that attempt to persuade readers that overeating is bad for your health. After each statement, indicate who you think the intended audience is:

- Parents
- Children
- Health professionals (doctors, nurses, dieticians)
- A person trying to lose weight

Statement #1:

"Cookies aren't the only yummy snack. Next time your tummy is empty, try an apple."

Intended Audience: _____

Statement #2:

"Difficult as it can be to say 'no' to requests for chips and candy, it is critical to remember that eating patterns are set early and that bad habits acquired in childhood can persist for life."

Intended Audience: _____

Statement #3:

"Think about why you reach for food with high caloric content. Ask yourself, ' Am I really hungry or am I depressed, bored, tired, or anxious?' Rather than getting to the cause of these feelings, an extra helping often only makes you feel worse because on top of the other feelings you now feel guilt."

Intended Audience: _____

Statement #4:

"Dr. Tistaert and his colleagues at Johns Hopkins University researched the effect of artificial sweeteners (aspartame) on overweight women. In a sample of 500 women examined over the course of three years, aspartame was found to assist both with weight loss as well as with long-term maintenance of a healthier body weight. For additional information on the study, see references at the bottom of the page."

Intended Audience: _____

Notice how the intended audience shaped the writer's word choice and sentence structure.

There is no need to guess what a teacher will be looking for in your essay. Most college instructors use a **rubric** similar to the one below to evaluate student writing. As you read your draft, consider changes you can make to make your finished essay match the description in category 5.

For the moment, focus on content and tone. You will work on grammar and mechanics during the editing process in the following lesson.

PERSUASIVE WRITING RUBRIC (5-point scale)

A 5 persuasive essay presents a convincing and insightful argument. The writer takes a position and supports it with carefully chosen and compelling evidence that appeals to both logic and emotions. The writer explains important opposing arguments and offers strong rebuttals. The essay is focused, demonstrates a clear sense of purpose and audience, and uses appropriate tone and style. Organization is coherent with appropriate transitions between and within paragraphs. Word choice is precise, sentences are varied, and grammatical errors are rare or absent.

A 4 persuasive essay presents a well-defined argument. The writer takes a position and supports it with sufficient evidence. The writer offers counter-arguments. The essay generally maintains its focus and demonstrates a sense of purpose, tone, and audience. Organization is generally clear with transitions between paragraphs. A competency with language is apparent. Word choice is appropriate and sentences are sometimes varied. Some errors in sentence structure, usage, and mechanics are present.

A 3 persuasive essay presents a minimally defined argument. The writer takes a position and attempts to support this position, but the evidence is underdeveloped and only partially elaborated. The writer may mention opposing arguments, but the rebuttal is weak or absent. The essay generally maintains its focus but may occasionally stray off topic. Its sense of purpose, tone, and audience may be inconsistent or unclear. Organization is clear enough to follow. A limited control of language is apparent. Word choice is imprecise, and sentences may be poorly constructed or confusing. Errors in sentence structure, usage, and mechanics are present.

A 2 persuasive essay presents a weakly developed argument. The writer takes a position but offers minimal and/or inappropriate evidence to support its claim. The essay demonstrates significant problems in one or more of the following areas which make the writer's ideas difficult to follow: unclear focus, lack of organization, weak thesis, and redundancy. Style and tone may be inappropriate for the audience. Writing demonstrates weak control of language. Errors in grammar and mechanics significantly interfere with meaning.

A 1 persuasive essay presents an ineffective argument. The writer may fail to take a position or offer only poorly chosen evidence to support the claim. Ideas and explanations are absent, irrelevant, unsupported by evidence, or incomprehensible. The essay lacks focus and organization, making the writer's ideas difficult to follow. Style and tone may be inappropriate for the audience. Writing demonstrates poor control of language. Errors in grammar and mechanics are pervasive and obstruct meaning.

Try It

I am attempting to persuade a reader that _____

_____.

The intended audience for this paper is/are _____

_____, whose attitude towards this issue is likely to be _____

_____

_____.

I would like the tone of my paper to be (circle all that apply):

friendly	sarcastic	angry	pessimistic
authoritative	straightforward	enthusiastic	instructive
humorous	thoughtful	sincere	optimistic
ironic	urgent	irate	informal
somber	dismayed	matter-of-fact	reasoned
cynical	earnest	critical	shocking
cautious	contemplative	scholarly	serious
candid	bemused	forthright	insistent
respectful	accusatory	harsh	concerned

Reread your draft. You may find it helpful to read your paper aloud, even to yourself. Most people are quite accomplished at presenting an argument in conversation. The challenge is to be equally effective on paper. As you read, mark places in your draft where:

1. **You need to include stronger supporting evidence.** If there is any room for someone to ask "why" or "how," then you have not been thorough enough in your explanation. Try to anticipate the questions your audience might have and answer them.

2. **Your tone is inappropriate for your audience.** If you are writing an academic paper, your tone should be serious. Consider giving your paper as a speech. Imagine how you would sound. That is how your paper should sound.

3. **You feel your choice of words is weak.** Avoid using words like "a lot" and "some." Be specific. Using phrases like "I think" and "in my opinion" weaken your argument. Don't mitigate or qualify your statements. The most convincing arguments are the most confident ones.

4. **You find yourself stumbling over a sentence.** Often you stumble because your sentence is too complex. If this is the case, simplify. A short sentence can be just as or even more powerful than a long one.

5. **Your meaning is unclear.** Sometimes writers lose the natural progression of the argument because they are focusing too much on the writing. If at any point it is unclear how what you are saying supports your main thesis statement, go back and clarify.

Once you have identified places in your draft that need revising, go back and improve these sections. This graphic organizer will help you decide what to do to make improvements.

IF	THEN
Your supporting evidence needs strengthening . . .	• Conduct additional research for more supporting data or expert testimony.
Your tone is inappropriate or too conversational for your audience . . .	• Replace slang phrasings like *awesome* and *incredible* with more formal expressions. • Eliminate all contractions (instead of *would've*, write *would have*).
Your word choice is weak or sounds babyish . . .	• Replace general nouns like *thing* and *stuff* with concrete, specific words. • Replace weak verbs like *do* and *get* with more vivid and more academic verbs like *engage, acquire, develop, convey*, and *conduct*.
Your sentences are clumsy or awkwardly constructed . . .	• Break down long, confusing sentences into simple sentences. • Combine short, choppy sentences into longer, more complex sentences. • Rephrase sentences for clarity.
Your meaning is unclear . . .	• Before attempting to correct a confusing sentence, restate the point you are trying to make out loud. We often speak more clearly than we write.

Most college professors expect papers to be handed in as typed copies. If you have access to a computer, type a new draft that incorporates your revisions. If you do not have a computer at hand, revise your essay on your own paper.

KNOW IT! Revision is the process of rereading a text and making changes in content, organization, sentence structure, and word choice in order to improve it.

Definitions to remember:

- **Tone:** a writer's attitude towards the subject
- **Audience:** the intended readers of the essay
- **Voice:** the writer's style as demonstrated through word choice and sentence structure

LESSON 6 Editing

Sentence **fragments** and **run-on sentences** are two of the most common errors in writing. You should **edit** your draft carefully for these sentence-level mistakes. Sentence variety, however, is a key feature of good writing. A crisp, short sentence can be a powerful way to make a point. Long, complex sentences are often needed to express complicated ideas. This lesson will help you learn how to employ both types of sentences correctly.

Sentences must have a **subject** and a **verb** and be a complete thought, capable of standing alone. If you construct a sentence that does not contain a subject or a main verb, what you have written is a fragment of a sentence.

Fragment: Gas-guzzling vehicles in the city. (missing a verb)

Corrected Sentence: Gas-guzzling vehicles <u>are out of place</u> in the city.

Fragment: Run on two cylinders. (missing a subject)

Corrected Sentence: <u>The most fuel-efficient cars</u> run on two cylinders.

For more information on **fragments** and **run-ons**, see p. 218.

A run-on sentence occurs when two complete sentences are constructed as though they were a single sentence.

Run-on: Gas-guzzling vehicles are expensive to drive it can cost over fifty dollars to fill a tank.

There are four basic ways to correct a run-on.

1. Insert a period.

- Gas-guzzling vehicles are expensive to drive. It can cost over fifty dollars to fill a tank.

2. Insert a semicolon. Used in the same was as periods, semicolons are used to join two or more closely related independent **clauses**.

- Gas-guzzling vehicles are expensive to drive; it can cost over fifty dollars to fill a tank.

3. Combine sentences with a comma and a coordinating conjunction (*for, and, nor, but, or, yet, so*).

- Gas-guzzling vehicles are expensive to drive, and can cost over fifty dollars to fill a tank.

4. Rewrite the sentence using a subordinating conjunction. These conjunctions make one of the two clauses dependent on the other. Common subordinating conjunctions include:

because	when	although
since	while	even though
so that	until	if
before	since	unless

- Gas-guzzling vehicles are expensive to drive <u>because</u> it can cost over fifty dollars to fill a tank.

EXAMPLE

Look at these examples of fragments and run-on sentences. On the lines that follow, explain what is wrong with the examples and how the errors can be corrected.

1. Bought a hybrid car and likes it very much.

   _____

   _____

2. Car manufacturers offer a narrow range of choices, buyers have few options when it comes to fuel-efficient vehicles.

   _____

   _____

3. Four-cylinder vehicles for buyers looking for better gas mileage.

   _____

   _____

4. Gas station owners insist they aren't getting rich and cab drivers are watching their profits dwindle.

   _____

   _____

Explanation of Examples

1. This is a fragment because there is no subject. Who bought the car? The error can be corrected by adding a subject.
   Corrected Sentence: Ana bought a hybrid car and likes it very much.

2. This is a run-on sentence; it includes two complete ideas expressed as one sentence. The error can be corrected in several different ways:
   - by splitting the run-on into two sentences with a period.

[TIP]

Remember, the subject tells who or what the sentence is about. The verb tells what the subject is doing.

[TIP]

If you are working on a computer and have the grammar check turned on, you will notice that the program automatically underlines sentence errors with a green line. While you never want to ignore a warning from grammar check, there may be times when you decide to use a fragment or run-on intentionally for effect.

Corrected Sentence: Car manufacturers offer a narrow range of choices. Buyers have few options when it comes to fuel-efficient vehicles.

- by adding an coordinating conjunction after the comma between the two clauses. Without adding this conjunction, the error is called a **comma splice**.
    Corrected Sentence: Car manufacturers offer a narrow range of choices, so buyers have few options when it comes to fuel-efficient vehicles.

- by inserting a semicolon between the two independent clauses.
    Corrected Sentence: Car manufacturers offer a narrow range of choices; buyers have few options when it comes to fuel-efficient vehicles.

3. This is a fragment because there is no verb. What about the four-cylinder vehicles? The error can be corrected by adding a verb.
    Corrected Sentence: Four-cylinder vehicles are perfect for buyers looking for better gas mileage.

4. This is a run-on because the sentence needs a comma after "rich" to separate the two independent clauses.
    Corrected Sentence: Gas station owners insist they aren't getting rich, and cab drivers are watching their profits dwindle.

Another way to correct this error and improve the sentence might be to rephrase it using a subordinating conjunction.
    Corrected Sentence: Although gas station owners insist they aren't getting rich, cab drivers' profits are dwindling.

Sentence Combining

If you find that many of your sentences sound short and choppy, try combining them into longer, more complex sentences. For example, the following three short sentences might be combined into a more interesting sentence. Learning how to construct complex sentences will make your writing more sophisticated.

Short, choppy sentences:
- Japanese cars are fuel-efficient.
- Japanese automakers design attractive cars that are safe.
- Americans are buying more and more Japanese cars.

Longer, more sophisticated sentence:
    In their search for attractive, safe, and fuel-efficient cars, more and more Americans are buying Japanese imports.

Practice this **sentence combining** technique by joining the following sets of short sentences to create longer, more complex sentences. Be careful not to create a run-on sentence as you weave the short sentences together. Remember there are different types of conjunctions (coordinating and subordinating) and that the punctuation rules differ for each.

Sentence Combining Practice Set #1

Too many cars on the road contain only one driver.
Fuel is wasted when people don't share rides.
Carpool lanes encourage ride sharing.

_____

_____

_____

Sentence Combining Practice Set #2

Trips to the gas station can be depressing.
The price of gas keeps going up.
Filling the tank takes a big bite out of one's paycheck.
Car owners need to rethink their priorities.

_____

_____

_____

Sentence Combining Practice Set #3

Cities should invest in mass transportation.
A bus, subway, or train can provide an alternative to cars.
Roads would be less crowded if fewer people drove.
You don't need to commute alone.

_____

_____

_____

[TIP]

Short sentences can be very effective. Experiment with a three-word sentence as a powerful first or last line in your persuasive essay. A short sentence can be a dramatic tool to attract readers' attention to your message.

Possible combined sentence #1: Carpool lanes encourage many single drivers to stop wasting fuel by sharing rides.

Possible combined sentence #2: As gas prices go up, drivers find it depressing that filling their tanks is taking a big bite out of their paychecks; many find they must rethink their priorities.

Possible combined sentence #3: Cities should invest in mass transit so that commuters have viable alternatives to driving alone on crowded highways.

Try It

[TIP]

Most writers generate many more than two drafts. The revising and editing processes often need to be revisited again and again until you are satisfied with what you have written—or until your paper is due!

Good writers have developed sentence sense: they use a variety of sentences—both short and long—in a way that enhances the effectiveness of their writing. A good way to develop your sentence sense is to analyze your own writing to discover what kinds of sentences you use most often. Are most of your sentences three or four words long? Are most of your sentences five or six lines long? If either is the case, your writing lacks sentence variety. The following exercise will also draw your attention to places where you have written fragments or run-ons.

Take a marker or highlighter and highlight or draw a line under the first sentence of your revised draft. Then use a second color marker or highlighter and do the same to the second sentence. Continue alternating colors to highlight or underline every sentence in your draft. This technique allows you to visually see how long your sentences are. Make sure that you have a variety of short and long sentences. Then follow these two steps:

1. Check for subjects and verbs in every sentence. If one or the other is missing, add what is needed to make the fragment a complete sentence.

2. Check long sentences for missing punctuation. Did you forget to insert a comma before the *and* or *but* in a long sentence? Would a semicolon be appropriate to use? Might the sentence be improved if you rewrote it? Would your sentences carry more impact if you split them into two shorter sentences with a period?

Edit your persuasive essay for grammar, mechanics, and **usage**. Be on the lookout for fragments and run-on sentences. If you use a spell-check program, be careful that the replacement it suggests is the word you want.

KNOW IT!

Fragments are incomplete sentences; they lack either a subject or a verb. Fragments can be used for effect, but often short, complete sentences are equally effective. Run-ons occur when two complete sentences are incorrectly written as one. Run-ons can be corrected by splitting the sentence into two complete sentences, correcting the punctuation that combines the sentences, or rewriting the sentence to make the relationship more clear.

It is important to thoroughly edit your draft before turning it in. Your message is clearer and more effective when the writing is clean.

Wrap It Up

Use the rubric below (introduced in lesson 1.5) to evaluate your essay before handing it in.

PERSUASIVE WRITING RUBRIC (5-point scale)

A 5 persuasive essay presents a convincing and insightful argument. The writer takes a position and supports it with carefully chosen and compelling evidence that appeals to both logic and emotions. The writer explains important opposing arguments and offers strong rebuttals. The essay is focused, demonstrates a clear sense of purpose and audience, and uses appropriate tone and style. Organization is coherent with appropriate transitions between and within paragraphs. Word choice is precise, sentences are varied, and grammatical errors are rare or absent.

A 4 persuasive essay presents a well-defined argument. The writer takes a position and supports it with sufficient evidence. The writer offers counter-arguments. The essay generally maintains its focus and demonstrates a sense of purpose, tone, and audience. Organization is generally clear with transitions between paragraphs. A competency with language is apparent. Word choice is appropriate and sentences are sometimes varied. Some errors in sentence structure, usage, and mechanics are present.

A 3 persuasive essay presents a minimally defined argument. The writer takes a position and attempts to support this position, but the evidence is underdeveloped and only partially elaborated. The writer may mention opposing arguments, but the rebuttal is weak or absent. The essay generally maintains its focus but may occasionally stray off topic. Its sense of purpose, tone, and audience may be inconsistent or unclear. Organization is clear enough to follow. A limited control of language is apparent. Word choice is imprecise, and sentences may be poorly constructed or confusing. Errors in sentence structure, usage, and mechanics are present.

A 2 persuasive essay presents a weakly developed argument. The writer takes a position but offers minimal and/or inappropriate evidence to support its claim. The essay demonstrates significant problems in one or more of the following areas which make the writer's ideas difficult to follow: unclear focus, lack of organization, weak thesis, and redundancy. Style and tone may be inappropriate for the audience. Writing demonstrates weak control of language. Errors in grammar and mechanics significantly interfere with meaning.

A 1 persuasive essay presents an ineffective argument. The writer may fail to take a position or offer only poorly chosen evidence to support the claim. Ideas and explanations are absent, irrelevant, unsupported by evidence, or incomprehensible. The essay lacks focus and organization, making the writer's ideas difficult to follow. Style and tone may be inappropriate for the audience. Writing demonstrates poor control of language. Errors in grammar and mechanics are pervasive and obstruct meaning.

My paper should score a: _____

Take a moment before turning in your paper to answer the following questions. This process will help you make you more aware of what to do the next time you need to write a persuasive essay.

1. To what extent did the final product match your expectations? If you are disappointed in the result, what is it about the finished product that you feel is weak and needs additional work?

_____

_____

_____

_____

_____

_____

_____

2. Did you care about the issue you tackled or did you lose interest? If you lost interest, what do you think was the problem? When you go to write another persuasive essay, what will you look for in a topic?

_____

_____

_____

_____

_____

_____

_____

3. What do you think is the most valuable use of persuasive writing? Explain.

_____

_____

_____

_____

_____

_____

UNIT 2 Writing to Explain

Have you ever tried to explain something to a friend? We do this all the time in conversation. In writing this process is called exposition. While the steps to composing such an essay may at first seem more involved, the intent is the same: to explain something to someone. In college you will be expected to write expository essays and research reports for many of the courses you take. On the job you may have to write incident reports, business letters, or employee evaluations. **Expository writing** is a skill you want to master—and not only for a grade. In your life after college, a promotion could depend on it!

When choosing a topic for your expository essay, try to select a subject you genuinely want to learn more about. You will be reading a great deal about this topic in the course of your research, so the more interested you are in the subject, the easier the work will seem. You will also find that you write more clearly and coherently when you care about the subject you are explaining to others. Are you a sports fan with concerns about the recruiting process or the salaries paid to top athletes? Are you worried about changing weather patterns and global warming? Are you interested in movies and the popularity of particular types of films or stars? Ultimately you will be presenting your topic—as well as what you think about it—to your readers.

Expository writing involves presenting information in a manner that demonstrates what you have learned and that helps others understand the topic. Two important skills you need to successfully do this are paraphrasing and summarizing. A **paraphrase** is a writer's attempt to restate in his or her own words what another author has said. When you paraphrase, you should:

- replace unfamiliar words in the original text with words you and your reader know.
- rewrite long, complex sentences into simpler sentences that are easier to understand.

Although quoting directly from a source can be effective in an expository essay, often you will need to take what you have discovered in your research and rephrase it into your own words. This will demonstrate to your readers that you know what you are talking about.

A **summary** is a brief statement of the main ideas and important details presented in a piece of text. Summaries should:

- be shorter than the original text.
- include the main events, ideas, or images.
- reflect the structure and order of the text.
- address underlying meaning rather than superficial details.

As you conduct research on a subject, you will collect much more information than you can include in your essay. You will need to summarize what others have said by including short, clear restatements of your findings in supporting paragraphs.

[TIP]

To read the entire essay of "The Pleasure of Writing," turn to page 51.

EXAMPLE—PARAPHRASING

Read the following excerpt from "The Pleasure of Writing" by A.A. Milne and the paraphrase that follows it. (You may already know this author from his *Winnie the Pooh* books.) Notice how the paraphrase restates the writer's sentence in simpler language while including both the main idea and details.

Original:

Sometimes when the printer is waiting for an article which really should have been sent to him the day before, I sit at my desk and wonder if there is any possible subject in the whole world upon which I can possibly find anything to say. On one such occasion I left it to Fate, which decided, by means of a dictionary opened at random, that I should deliver myself of a few thoughts about goldfish.

Sample Paraphrase: *Sometimes when I have a deadline to meet and am late sending in my essay, I sit and try to think of what I can possibly write about. One time I just opened the dictionary and randomly chose a word for my subject. The word I picked for that article was "goldfish."*

■ Try It—Paraphrasing

Paraphrase the following sentence from "The Pleasure of Writing." Remember, the goal of your paraphrase is to demonstrate your understanding of the sentence in your own words.

Original:

When poets and idiots talk of the pleasure of writing, they mean the pleasure of giving a piece of their minds to the public; with an old nib a tedious business.

Paraphrase: _____

_____

_____

_____

_____

_____

_____

_____

A nib is the metal writing tip of an old-fashioned pen, and *tedious* means "tiresome."

Check your work:

  1. Does your paraphrase express the main idea of the original sentence?

  2. Does your paraphrase include the details expressed in the original sentence?

If you answered *no* to either of these questions, revise your paraphrase.

Now that you have a feel for how paraphrasing works, paraphrase the following long sentence from the same article. It is perfectly acceptable to use two or three short sentences in your paraphrase of a complex sentence.

Original:

> But if there be one compositor not carried away by the mad rush of life, who in a leisurely hour (the luncheon one, for instance) looks at the beautiful words with the eye of an artist, not of a wage-earner, he, I think, will be satisfied; he will be as glad as I am of my new nib.

Paraphrase: _____

_____

_____

_____

_____

_____

[TIP]

A compositor is a typesetter, someone who takes a writer's handwritten manuscript and sets it into print.

EXAMPLE—SUMMARIZING

Presenting information clearly and coherently can be a challenge for anyone composing an expository essay. The temptation to cut and paste whole passages from Internet sources is enormous. So is the danger. The punishment for **plagiarism** can be severe. You could find yourself with an automatic F in the class or even in danger of expulsion. Moreover, most writing assignments for college have a page limit. You don't have room in your paper for all the information you find on your subject. You will need to summarize.

Read this paragraph from "The Pleasure of Writing" and the sample summary that follows. Notice how the summary focuses on only the main idea and most important details.

Original:

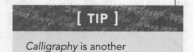
[TIP]

Calligraphy is another word for handwriting.

> A woman, who had studied what she called the science of calligraphy, once offered to tell my character from my handwriting. I prepared a special sample for her; it was full of sentences like "To be good is to be happy," "Faith is the lode-star of life," "We should always be kind to animals," and so on. I wanted her to do her best. She gave the morning to it, and told me at lunch that I was "synthetic." Probably you think that the compositor has failed me here and printed "synthetic" when I wrote "sympathetic." In just this way I misunderstood my calligraphist at first, and I looked as sympathetic as I could. However, she repeated "synthetic,"

so that there could be no mistake. I begged her to tell me more, for I had thought that every letter would reveal a secret, but all she would add was "and not analytic." I went about for the rest of the day saying proudly to myself "I am synthetic! I am synthetic! I am synthetic!" and then I would add regretfully, "Alas, I am not analytic!" I had no idea what it meant.

Sample summary: *Once the author had his handwriting analyzed by someone who claimed she could tell his character from the way he shaped his letters. Her response made no sense to the author, and he mocked it.*

Try It—Summarizing

Read the following paragraph from "The Pleasure of Writing" and write a short summary on the lines that follow. For the sake of discipline, try to use fewer than 25 words. Remember that a summary focuses on the main idea and most important details and omits the smaller, unimportant details.

Original:

The nib I write this with is called the "Canadian Quill"; made, I suppose, from some steel goose which flourishes across the seas, and which Canadian housewives have to explain to their husbands every Michaelmas. Well, it has seen me to the end of what I wanted to say—if indeed I wanted to say anything. For it was enough for me this morning just to write; with spring coming in through the open windows and my good Canadian quill in my hand, I could have copied out a directory. That is the real pleasure of writing.

Summary: _____

_____

_____

_____

_____

_____

_____

Check your work:

1. Does your summary convey the main idea of the passage?

2. Is your summary significantly shorter than the original?

If you answered *no* to either of these questions, revise your summary.

[TIP]

Michaelmas is a feast day on which goose is traditionally served like turkey at Thanksgiving.

[TIP]

When attempting to summarize a long passage, pay particular attention to the first and last sentences of paragraphs. Clues to the author's main idea can often be found there.

Brainstorming a Topic

Now that you have practiced paraphrasing and summarizing, it is time to decide on a topic for your expository essay. What are you curious about? Take a trip to your local library or bookstore and notice what titles attract your attention. Flip through news magazines to find issues that seem important to you. Check out the listings of educational television programming to discover topics that seem engaging. The possibilities are endless!

Use the following lines to **brainstorm** topics for your expository essay. Write down words, phrases, or ideas that interest you. They don't have to be related to each other. When brainstorming, think about what you like to talk about with your friends, what news stories interest you, and what kinds of things you enjoy reading about. Try to brainstorm for at least five minutes before stopping to look back over your list.

_____   _____

_____   _____

_____   _____

_____   _____

_____   _____

_____   _____

_____   _____

If you're struggling to come up with a topic on your own, the following list may give you ideas about the kinds of topics that are likely to result in engaging expository essays.

Ideas for expository essays

- Childhood Obesity: Causes, Effects, and Solutions
- Global Warming: Fact or Fantasy?
- How Electronic Gaming Is Shaping Young Minds
- What's Wrong with Public Education
- National Health Care: An Idea Whose Time Has Come
- Homelessness in America
- Sports Heroes: Why So Many Find Themselves in Trouble
- Pets and the Elderly: Taking Care
- How has technology affected American lives and lifestyles?
- Intellectual Property Rights: Should Music Be Free?
- The History of Vampires
- Civil Rights Issues in the Twenty-First Century
- What will it take to make and keep our homeland safe?

Before moving on to the next lesson, choose a subject for your expository essay and find at least four sources of information from the library or online. Turn back to Unit 1, Lesson 2 for reminders about taking notes as you read.

KNOW IT! When writing an expository essay, you will often need to paraphrase and summarize information. Remember, a summary is always shorter than the original, while a paraphrase can be as long as or longer than the original. A summary focuses only on main ideas and the most important details, while a paraphrase includes all of the details, big and small. Both summaries and paraphrases are written in your own words. Even though the information is expressed in your own words, you must still give credit to your sources. Keep notes of where you found information and cite your sources.

The Pleasure of Writing
By A. A. Milne

Sometimes when the printer is waiting for an article which really should have been sent to him the day before, I sit at my desk and wonder if there is any possible subject in the whole world upon which I can possibly find anything to say. On one such occasion I left it to Fate, which decided, by means of a dictionary opened at random, that I should deliver myself of a few thoughts about goldfish. (You will find this article later on in the book.) But to-day I do not need to bother about a subject. To-day I am without a care. Nothing less has happened than that I have a new nib in my pen.

In the ordinary way, when Shakespeare writes a tragedy, or Mr. Blank gives you one of his charming little essays, a certain amount of thought goes on before pen is put to paper. One cannot write "Scene I. An Open Place. Thunder and Lightning. Enter Three Witches," or "As I look up from my window, the nodding daffodils beckon to me to take the morning," one cannot give of one's best in this way on the spur of the moment. At least, others cannot. But when I have a new nib in my pen, then I can go straight from my breakfast to the blotting-paper, and a new sheet of foolscap fills itself magically with a stream of blue-black words. When poets and idiots talk of the pleasure of writing, they mean the pleasure of giving a piece of their minds to the public; with an old nib a tedious business. They do not mean (as I do) the pleasure of the artist in seeing beautifully shaped "k's" and sinuous "s's" grow beneath his steel. Anybody else writing this article might wonder "Will my readers like it?" I only tell myself "How the compositors will love it!"

But perhaps they will not love it. Maybe I am a little above their heads. I remember on one First of January receiving an anonymous postcard wishing me a happy New Year, and suggesting that I should give the compositors a happy New Year also by writing more generously. In those days I got a thousand words upon one sheet 8 in. by 5 in. I adopted the suggestion, but it was a wrench; as it would be for a painter of miniatures forced to spend the rest of his life painting the Town Council of Boffington in the manner of Herkomer. My canvases are bigger now, but they are still impressionistic. "Pretty, but what is it?" remains the obvious comment; one steps back a pace and saws the air with the hand; "You see it better from here, my love," one says to one's wife. But if there be one compositor not carried away by the mad rush of life, who in a leisurely hour (the luncheon one, for instance) looks at the beautiful words with the eye of an artist, not of a wage-earner, he, I think, will be satisfied; he will be as glad as I am of my new nib. Does it matter, then, what you who see only the printed word think of it?

A woman, who had studied what she called the science of calligraphy, once offered to tell my character from my handwriting. I prepared a special sample for her; it was full of sentences like "To be good is to be happy," "Faith is the lode-star of life," "We should always be kind to animals," and so on. I wanted her to do her best. She gave the morning to it, and told me at lunch that I was "synthetic." Probably you think that the compositor has failed me here and printed "synthetic" when I wrote "sympathetic." In just this way I misunderstood my calligraphist at first, and I looked as sympathetic as I could. However, she repeated "synthetic," so that there could be no mistake. I begged her to tell me more, for I had thought that every letter would reveal a secret, but all she would add was "and not analytic." I went about for the rest of the day saying proudly to myself "I am synthetic! I am synthetic! I am synthetic!" and then I would add regretfully, "Alas, I am not analytic!" I had no idea what it meant.

And how do you think she had deduced my syntheticness? Simply from the fact that, to save time, I join some of my words together. That isn't being synthetic, it is being in a hurry. What she should have said was, "You are a busy man; your life is one constant whirl; and probably you are of excellent moral character and kind to animals." Then one would feel that one did not write in vain.

My pen is getting tired; it has lost its first fair youth. However, I can still go on. I was at school with a boy whose uncle made nibs. If you detect traces of erudition in this article, of which any decent man might be expected to be innocent, I owe it to that boy. He once told me how many nibs his uncle made in a year; luckily I have forgotten. Thousands, probably. Every term that boy came back with a hundred of them; one expected him to be very busy. After all, if you haven't the brains or the inclination to work, it is something to have the nibs. These nibs, however, were put to better uses. There is a game you can play with them; you flick your nib against the other boy's nib, and if a lucky shot puts the head of yours under his, then a sharp tap capsizes him, and you have a hundred and one in your collection. There is a good deal of strategy in the game (whose finer points I have now forgotten), and I have no doubt that they play it at the Admiralty in the off season. Another game was to put a clean nib in your pen, place it lightly against the cheek of a boy whose head was turned away from you, and then call him suddenly. As Kipling says, we are the only really humorous race. This boy's uncle died a year or two later and left about £80,000, but none of it to his nephew. Of course, he had had the nibs every term. One mustn't forget that.

The nib I write this with is called the "Canadian Quill"; made, I suppose, from some steel goose which flourishes across the seas, and which Canadian housewives have to explain to their husbands every Michaelmas. Well, it has seen me to the end of what I wanted to say—if indeed I wanted to say anything. For it was enough for me this morning just to write; with spring coming in through the open windows and my good Canadian quill in my hand, I could have copied out a directory. That is the real pleasure of writing.

LESSON 2 Organizing Your Ideas

A thesis statement explains what point you will be making in your essay. It always appears as a complete sentence and states your position or attitude toward your subject. For example, "childhood obesity" is a topic; your proposal of a solution to prevent childhood obesity is your thesis. All the evidence presented in your expository essay—your explanation of the problem, your description of worst-case scenarios, the testimony of medical experts—should be organized around your thesis statement. Solid supporting evidence *exposes* the truth of your thesis. That's why it's called an expository essay!

Your thesis statement provides a road map for the rest of your essay, guiding readers through the paper by highlighting what is most important. In an expository essay, your thesis statement may or may not appear as the first sentence. Often writers choose to present an engaging introduction—possibly an anecdote or a surprising statistic—that engages readers in the subject before presenting the all-important thesis statement. Rather than worrying about writing this introduction first, focus on the big idea you want readers to take away from the essay. Your ultimate goal is to explain the material so thoroughly and convincingly that readers find your thesis self-evident.

Often college essay exams pose questions that you are expected to answer using material you learned in the course. Given that you are likely to be working under the pressure of time and that your reader will be looking for a correct answer to the question, for exams it is best to address the prompt directly in your very first sentence. This will become your thesis statement, and stating it up front lets your examiner know that you understand what is being asked. What follows in your essay demonstrates your mastery of the material.

Crafting an effective thesis statement can be a challenge, particularly if you are still in the process of doing research for your essay and gathering supporting evidence. To help give shape to your reading and research, try writing a working thesis statement. This draft thesis may well change as you discover new information or even rethink your own position on the subject, but having a working thesis as a place to start will help you to maintain your focus as you draft your expository essay.

EXAMPLE

What makes an effective working thesis? One that is specific enough to provide focus for your expository essay without being so narrow that you quickly run out of things to write about. Let's use the topic of childhood obesity as an example. A working thesis for an expository essay exploring the causes, effects, and solutions to the problem might read something like:

Childhood obesity is a growing national problem that every responsible parent should be committed to preventing.

This working thesis allows the writer to offer evidence supporting the claim that childhood obesity is a "growing national problem," as well as to develop the argument that responsible parents must act to prevent their children from becoming obese. There is room in this thesis for elaboration of causes, effects, and solutions.

You should avoid vague thesis statements that present simplistic expressions of the topic like, "There are many reasons why childhood obesity is bad for America's children." It is hard to tell from this thesis what the writer's attitude towards the subject is. A narrow thesis like, "It's hard for children to lose weight once they have gained it by eating too much candy" limits the scope of the essay.

Researching Your Topic

Few writers can produce an expository essay off the top of their heads. To write a compelling paper, you will need to do some research on your topic, gathering evidence—facts, data, anecdotes, and expert opinions—that supports your topic and the position you may be taking on your subject. As you research, keep each piece of evidence on a separate note card, along with its source. This will help you organize your points later and make it easier to create a Works Cited page.

As you search for information in books, magazines, and on the Internet, you need to evaluate your sources. Not every piece of evidence or set of statistics is equally valuable. Here are some guidelines that can help you make good decisions about the reliability and applicability of what you find:

[TIP]

Summarizing Your Research
Once you have found information you plan to use in your expository essay, use the summarizing skills you learned in Lesson 1 of this unit to take notes. Remember to include in your notes all the information you will need later for a Works Cited page: author, title, publisher, date of publication, place of publication, page number, Web site address.

1. Check the biography of the author. Does the writer have the credentials and the authority to be trusted on this subject?

2. Check the credibility of the publisher. Was the article published by a university press or well-respected newspaper, or did it appear on a personal Web page or blog? Are you citing from the Web site of an established organization like the American Medical Association or the National Council of Teachers of Mathematics?

3. Check the date of publication. Is the information up to date?

4. Check for **bias**. Can you determine the context within which the information was written? Does the source of the information have a well-known point of view or bias?

5. Check that the information you cite is applicable to your thesis. You may find fascinating details that you would like to include for effect, but make sure every piece of evidence specifically advances your argument. Irrelevant details detract from the focus of your essay.

Sample Note Card:

Many children in America are eating far too much. The average
6-year-old should only be consuming as much meat as can fit in their
palm. When small children consume more calories than they burn off,
fat cells develop. Some of these fat cells remain with children their
entire lives.

Source: *Eating Healthy* by Jenny Salinger. Published by Norton in
New York in 2007. Information found on page 23.

Organizing Your Essay

The next step in crafting an effective expository essay is to create an organizational plan
for presenting your supporting evidence.

When explaining a scientific process or a historical event, you might organize your
essay chronologically. You discuss the steps or stages in their proper order, devoting
a paragraph to each step or stage.

For a **comparison/contrast essay**, you might decide to use either a **block method** or
point method. An essay organized using the block method presents the two things being
compared separately using the same set of criteria. For example, if you were comparing
and contrasting a novel and a film version of the novel, the organizational structure
employing the block method might look like this:

Paragraph #1—Introduction with thesis statement

Paragraph #2—Analysis of the novel *The Road* by Cormac McCarthy in terms
of its:

- Themes
- Characterization
- Impact on readers

Paragraph #3—Analysis of the film version of *The Road* in terms of its:

- Themes
- Characterization
- Impact on viewers

Paragraph #4—Conclusion synthesizing the comparison and contrast

An essay organized using the point method presents the two things being compared side
by side according to a set of **criteria**. If you were to use the point method for organizing
the same essay discussed above, the structure might look like this:

Paragraph #1—Introduction with thesis statement

Paragraph #2—Analysis of themes in the book compared with the themes in the film

Paragraph #3—Analysis of characterization in the book compared with characterization in the film

Paragraph #4—Analysis of the impact of the book on readers compared with the impact of the film on viewers

Paragraph #5—Conclusion synthesizing the comparison and contrast

For a **cause-and-effect essay** on childhood obesity, you might use an organizational plan like the one below.

Introductory Paragraph with working thesis statement—Childhood obesity is a growing national problem that every responsible parent should be committed to preventing.

Supporting Paragraph #1—The causes of childhood obesity

Supporting Paragraph #2—The effects of obesity on children's health

(Optional) Supporting Paragraph #3—Solutions to the problem

Concluding Paragraph—Discussion of the importance of addressing the problem now.

■ Try It

On the lines below draft a working thesis for the topic you have selected for your expository essay. Then ask yourself the following questions about your thesis:

- Is my thesis specific enough to interest readers in my topic or is it too vague?
- Does my thesis allow room for the development of a range of supporting evidence?
- Does the thesis present an argument that makes readers want to know more about this subject?

_____

_____

_____

_____

_____

_____

Don't be surprised if it takes you several attempts to come up with a working thesis that meets all of these criteria. Spending time crafting this statement is time well spent. Your thesis statement will be the keystone around which the rest of your essay will be built. You need it to be both strong and flexible, pointed yet roomy.

Planning Your Essay

Try using this graphic organizer to plan out your essay. Be sure that your supporting points follow one another logically.

Working thesis statement	
Supporting point #1	
Supporting point #2	
Supporting point #3	
Optional supporting point #4 or Conclusion	

Generating Topic Sentences for Supporting Paragraphs

[TIP]

Remember that each of your topic sentences should follow from and support your thesis.

Just as your expository essay requires a powerful thesis statement to hold it together, each of your supporting paragraphs needs a strong topic sentence. Topic sentences state the main idea of the paragraph, directing the paragraph's development. For example, in the essay we have been working with on childhood obesity, the first supporting point is a discussion of causes. An effective topic sentence for this paragraph might be, "While some individuals may be genetically inclined to obesity, the majority of overweight children eat too much and exercise too little." This topic sentence could then be followed by details from your research about the kinds of food that commonly contribute to obesity, as well as a discussion about the eating habits and behavior patterns of overweight children.

Use the lines below to write topic sentences for each of your supporting points.

Topic Sentence for Supporting Paragraph #1

_____

_____

Topic Sentence for Supporting Paragraph #2

_____

_____

Lesson 2: *Organizing Your Ideas*   **57**

Topic Sentence for Supporting Paragraph #3

_____

_____

Topic Sentence for Supporting Paragraph #4 (optional)

_____

_____

If you're having a difficult time creating a topic sentence or identifying the main idea of a paragraph, you may be trying to include too much information in the paragraph. Try breaking the troublesome paragraph into two or more paragraphs that each present unique information.

Creating an Outline

It is important that your essay have a strong backbone. An **outline** can help make sure it does. An outline essentially serves as a map for you to follow when drafting your essay. Though you may depart from your outline as you draft, it is always a good idea to have a plan. Using the following as an example, create an outline of your expository essay on your own paper.

Thesis: _____

   I. Supporting point _____

      A. Example _____

      B. Evidence _____

      C. Commentary _____

   II. Supporting point _____

      A. Example _____

      B. Evidence _____

      C. Commentary _____

   III. Supporting point _____

      A. Example _____

      B. Evidence _____

      C. Commentary _____

KNOW IT! A thesis gives your readers an idea of what to expect in the essay as a whole. Similarly, topic sentences tell the reader what the main idea of each individual paragraph is. Both thesis statements and topic sentences help focus your essay and can help you identify when you are saying too much or not enough.

Working from a plan—a set of notes, a graphic organizer, an outline—will help you maintain the focus of your essay and keep you from straying from your thesis statement. Focus is an important element of all expository writing. What good is an explanation if it is hard to follow? Help your readers by sticking to a clear plan.

Before moving on, it is important to revisit and possibly revise your working thesis. If the backbone of your expository essay is weak, your essay will lack focus and be far less effective.

If your working thesis . . .	Then : . . .
Is too narrow to include some of the material you want to cite . . .	Rewrite your thesis to enlarge its scope.
Does not reveal your attitude towards the subject . . .	Revise your thesis to include your point of view on the subject you are exploring.
Seems vague or unfocused . . .	Sharpen your thesis statement so that it puts forward a compelling argument.

Revised Thesis Statement

_____

_____

_____

_____

_____

_____

_____

How to begin? It's a question that puzzles and frustrates every writer, no matter how experienced. You stare at the blank pages and worry that you will never fill them, that despite all your research you really don't know much about this topic and that readers will find you dull. You worry that you will make mistakes you have never even heard of. These feelings are natural. Trust that you can make your sentences sparkle later during revision. For this lesson simply set yourself the goal of getting your ideas down in as much detail as possible.

Drafting an expository essay begins with a deep breath. Try to relax and put aside concerns for perfection. Focus instead on expressing your ideas fully. Cutting weak sentences and eliminating repetition is easy compared with writing down what it is you have to say in the first place. Remind yourself why this topic interested you. If possible, talk with a friend about the subject. Explaining how you feel about the subject in an informal setting will help you gather and organize your thoughts. It may also help to dispel the terror of the blank page.

A common weakness of expository essays is a lack of **elaboration**. Elaboration is using descriptions, explanations, examples, and other details to thoroughly develop a point or idea. For each supporting **paragraph** you should try to develop your explanation in enough detail that a reader unfamiliar with your subject will learn from your essay and find your argument compelling. A paragraph is not simply a unit of length. Think of a paragraph as unit of thought that sets out a clear explanation of one aspect of your thesis. Each supporting paragraph should include (though not necessarily in this order):

- A topic sentence expressing your main idea

- An explanation or discussion of the main idea

- An example or piece of evidence

- Commentary on the example or piece of evidence

Some supporting paragraphs may contain more than one example. Be sure, though, that all the examples in a single paragraph are clearly related to your main idea.

Read the paragraph below, paying careful attention to how the writer develops the main idea presented in the topic sentence with examples, evidence, and commentary. The topic sentence has been underlined for you.

<u>While some individuals may be genetically inclined to obesity, most overweight children eat too much and exercise too little.</u> The problem is compounded when the foods growing children eat contain empty calories. Salty snacks like potato chips and sweet snacks like cookies may be tasty, but they provide little nutrition. The American Heart Association recommends that children between 4 and 8 years old consume between 1200–1400 calories per day. When a 16-ounce bottle of soda contains 200 calories, it is easy to see how easy it is to consume more calories than one needs. Carbonated beverages are also addictive and bad for children's teeth as well as for their waistlines. A steady diet of fast food is another cause of childhood obesity. A McDonald's® Happy Meal consisting of a child-sized cheeseburger, French fries, and soda contains 650 calories—over half of what an active child requires in a full day to maintain a healthy weight. No wonder youngsters who spend most of their time at a school desk or in front of the television are getting fat. With little chance for physical activity to burn off the extra calories they are consuming, they are bound to put on pounds.

When to Begin a New Paragraph

You should indent and begin a new paragraph:

1. To separate your introduction and conclusion from the rest of your essay.

2. Each time you introduce a new supporting point.

3. Whenever the essay takes a turn. For example, the writer of the preceding paragraph might want to include a second paragraph discussing additional causes of childhood obesity—fewer children walking to school, less time on the playground, the cutting of physical education classes, etc.

4. When a paragraph becomes so long that you feel readers need a visual break on the page. Though length alone should not determine the size of your paragraphs, it is rare that a single paragraph should go on for more than one page.

5. To distinguish among varying points of view. When citing experts or evidence from your research, separate differing opinions into distinct paragraphs. This will help readers follow your argument.

■ Try It

Below is an expository essay about fighting on high school campuses. It is reproduced here without paragraph breaks. See if you can determine where the writer originally chose to break for paragraphs. As you read, mark the places where you think each new paragraph would have begun.

[TIP]

See Common Editing Marks on p. 231 to identify how to mark a paragraph break.

Taking the Fight Out of Teenagers

The recent spate of disturbances on high school campuses across the city is just that—disturbing. What are all these teenagers fighting about? Why are they so angry? How is it that teenagers' fuses are so short? From Los Angeles Unified School District's Jefferson High School to Riverside's Norte Vista High School to Santa Monica High School, individual arguments are escalating into melees. Why? And what can adults do to stop it from happening? It is tempting to blame human nature. Kids have always fought and fights have always drawn a crowd. Running to catch the action, students' pulses race. Their eyes shine, wild with excitement. Pushing and shoving for front row views, bystanders contribute to the mayhem. It's a rush. While it isn't hard to see why teenagers would choose such a show over sitting in a desk doing geometry or reading *Julius Caesar*, school should be the one place in a child's life where reason and order prevail. The problem is that schools operate within the larger society, and when that society glorifies violent behavior it becomes increasingly difficult to maintain order in school. One has only to look around to see how teenagers are being lured astray: professional athletes attack their fans, hip-hop artists boast of violent crimes, reality shows reward aggression. If we want peace on school campuses, adults must examine our own complicity in providing and promoting entertainment that encourages the cave man within. Children need to be civilized. Socrates, not Tony Soprano, should be their role model.

Parents of 4-year-olds work hard to teach heated offspring to use words rather than hitting or biting to solve playground problems. The work can't stop with taking turns on the slide, though. Teenagers need to see adults in the media and in the news working through disputes without recourse to fisticuffs. While I applaud efforts of counselors to understand and sort out the conflicts between individuals and groups of students, I also feel that we will never be able to eliminate all the things that make teenagers mad. The hole my son punched in his bedroom wall when he was in high school serves as a reminder of the fury that smolders within many a young man upon receipt of the third speeding ticket or worse. Most grow out of this anger naturally and without doing lasting damage to themselves or others. In many ways 17-year-olds are children in men and women's bodies. We need to help them learn to deal with their anger as well as take responsibility for their mistakes. At campuses across the nation student scuffles are dealt with severely. Parents are called in. Suspensions are dealt out. Police are often summoned to restore order as well as impress upon students the seriousness of disturbing the peace. Along with these official repercussions, we must also teach teenagers the simple guidelines of getting along with others, even those we don't particularly like. Just as we taught our kindergarteners to stop, look, and listen before crossing the road, we need to teach our high school age children what to do the next time they feel the urge to raise their fists: stop, think, breathe, and walk away.

Let's see if you and the writer agree about the best places for paragraph breaks. In the original essay these were the first words of each paragraph:

Paragraph 1: The recent spate . . .

Paragraph 2: It is tempting . . .

Paragraph 3: The problem is . . .

Paragraph 4: Children need to be civilized.

Paragraph 5: While I applaud . . .

Paragraph 6: At campuses across the nation . . .

How well did you do? It is fairly easy to indentify the introductory and concluding paragraphs, but you may have had difficulty separating the supporting paragraphs from one another. Notice how the second paragraph first sentence ("It is tempting . . .") sets up an argument that the writer ultimately refutes, or disproves. With the statement "The problem is . . ." you find a clear topic sentence signaling a new paragraph. Paragraph 4's "Children need to be civilized" offers the beginning of the writer's proposed solution to the problem. Paragraph 5 offers a personal anecdote to illustrate the writer's thesis. While these paragraphs are not of equal length, each clearly marks a separate point in the writer's argument.

Expanding Sentences

Writing well takes practice. Consider how many scales a piano student needs to play every day to develop his or her skill or how many drills a soccer player runs in order to perform well in a game. An exercise that will help you practice developing your ideas is to expand basic sentences into longer, richer, more interesting, and more detailed sentences.

Example
Bare bones sentence: Kids eat too much candy.
Detailed sentence: Too often when children are hungry they reach for a candy bar like a Snickers® or Twix®.

Notice how the inclusion of brand names makes the image more concrete and invites the reader to relate specifically to the point you are making.

Expand the bare bones sentences below with details and concrete images. Try to make the detailed sentence at least twice as long as the original sentence.

Bare bones sentence: Children should get more exercise.

Detailed sentence: _____

_____

_____

Bare bones sentence: Overweight kids are often mocked.

Detailed sentence: _____

_____

_____

Bare bones sentence: Fruit is a better snack than chips.

Detailed sentence: _____

_____

_____

Bare bones sentence: It's hard to lose weight.

Detailed sentence: _____

_____

_____

Writing Your Draft

It is time to write. Following the plan set out in your graphic organizer from the previous lesson, draft your essay. Remember, don't worry about finding the perfect word or phrasing for every sentence. Just get your ideas down on paper. Make sure to personally comment on every researched piece of evidence you cite. The facts alone don't make your case for you—analysis of the facts will.

_____

_____

_____

_____

_____

_____

_____

_____

_____

_____

_____

_____

_____

_____

[TIP]

Remember to start a new paragraph whenever you begin to explain a new point in your essay.

_____

_____

_____

_____

_____

_____

_____

_____

_____

_____

_____

_____

_____

_____

_____

_____

_____

_____

 KNOW IT! When writing to explain, you teach something to your readers. The information you present will help others think more deeply and thoughtfully about a subject you care about.

 Before proceeding in this unit, reread your draft and ask yourself the following questions:

- Have I provided readers with a clear explanation of my thesis?

- Did I offer enough compelling evidence to support my thesis?

- Do I need to do additional research to strengthen my essay?

If you feel like your essay needs a little work, now is the time to do it. Keep drafting until you feel you have clearly communicated your ideas. Most writers write many drafts before they are satisfied enough to move on!

Have you ever noticed how much easier it is to recognize weaknesses and mistakes in someone else's work than in your own? Whether singing or writing, it is as though you just can't hear where you may have hit a wrong note. This lesson will help you refine your critical skills on another student's draft in order to improve your own.

The first thing to focus on when evaluating a draft is whether or not the essay achieves its purpose. Remember, the purpose of an expository essay is to explain an idea or process. A writer assumes that readers of the essay know something about the subject but may not have examined it carefully. Without talking down to the audience, writers of expository essays offer information, expert opinion, and facts that expand readers' understanding of an issue. Ideally the information is presented in a manner that readers find compelling. It is difficult to achieve your purpose if readers are bored and begin drifting off after the first few lines.

Use the following questions to help you determine whether or not an expository essay draft clearly explains an idea or process:

1. Does the writer generate interest for the subject in the opening paragraph?

2. Can a reader without specialized knowledge of the subject follow the argument presented in the essay?

3. Does the structure of the essay provide a strong framework for the content?

4. Do the ideas flow logically from one to the next?

5. Does the writer offer examples that make readers care about the issue?

6. Can you summarize what you have learned from the essay in a few sentences?

You should also be on the lookout for things that turn readers off and that suggest the writer does not have command of the subject or has overlooked something important in the presentation of ideas.

Weaknesses	Suggestions for Improvement
Use of specialized vocabulary that general readers would be unfamiliar with	Include definitions of unfamiliar terms or of words used in an unfamiliar context.
Including too many quotations	Paraphrase quotations. Direct quotations should not exceed 20% of the total words in an expository essay.
Unnecessary references to the writer (I think, I believe, Let me explain, etc.)	Delete first person references unless they clearly help readers engage with the writer on the issue.
Inclusion of rambling personal anecdotes	Include commentary to explain how this story relates to the essay's thesis.
Long lists of statistics or data	Present information more naturally and harmoniously into the body of the essay or within a chart.

EXAMPLE

Read the following draft of an expository essay. The student author is attempting to explain how American consumers should alter their eating and spending habits. Use the questions and comments provided to help you think about the essay's strengths as well as to make suggestions for improvement.

The Consumer Corrects Industrial Flaws Because Executives Do Not

In "The Pleasures of Eating," Wendell Berry advises city people to eat responsibly in order to combat the decline in American farming and rural life. Eating responsibly can be described as furthering one's consciousness of one's participation in the agricultural system. ❷ Berry is clear that it is the eater's responsibility to resist becoming the unconscious and indifferent consumer that the food industry relies on to make a profit. I agree that the consumer must play a role in the reconstruction of the food industry, but I believe that the corporate executives must stop thinking with their wallets and help change the system as well.

Consumers can change the quality of products available to them. ❸ Consumers do this not by accusing big corporations of immoral actions, but by uniting and then altering their purchasing habits. A good example of this is the automobile industry and the current oil crisis. As gas prices soar, people are hesitant to buy the gas guzzling SUVs and trucks. People everywhere are looking into hybrid technology. The most popular hybrid available is Toyota's Prius. My dad is interested in purchasing the Prius but cannot, as he is only one of many environmentally conscious consumers on the

❶ Is this an effective title? Why or why not?

_____

_____

_____

❷ Without having read the Wendell Berry essay, readers would have no idea what the writer meant by "eating responsibly." It was an excellent idea to define this expression in the second sentence here.

❸ Is this an effective topic sentence? On the lines below, revise this student's topic sentence.

_____

_____

_____

_____

_____

4 This discussion of oil prices, hybrid cars, and waiting lists is off topic and could be confusing for a reader.

5 The repetition of the pronoun *one* in this paragraph feels awkward and distancing for the reader.

6 Does the concluding sentence relate everything back to the thesis of the essay?

7 Notice how this concluding sentence ties back to the main thesis of the essay: the role of consumers.

8 *Pleasant* seems too weak a word here. Can you think of a better word or phrase?

9 To make this a more powerful expository essay, the writer should use additional references.

two-month waiting list. **4** Consumers have power. If people ceased to buy food that was unhealthy for them, the fast food industry would have to reinvent their product.

If one does not want to be so reliant on the food industry, one can choose to tend a garden or farm, and thus have a personal food source. By tending a garden or farm, one strengthens the connection one feels with the land. **5** A garden is also a constant reminder that food does not come from the grocery store. A person who personally cares for a garden is guaranteed to be more environmentally conscious than the average city dweller. Harvesting and farming are both excellent ways to sever one's reliance on the food industry and to reestablish the broken bond between humans and the land. **6**

Another area where consumer spending influences the products offered for sale is in fast food services. By patronizing McDonalds and Taco Bell® where they consume quantities of processed, precooked foods that offer little in the way of nutrition, consumers contribute to a system where the range of foods being produced is narrowed, corporate profits soar, and their own health suffers. For these people, eating responsibly and following Berry's advice could make a difference not only for family nutrition but also for the long-term economic health of the land. Consumers need more nutritious options, but they also need to take responsibility for making better choices about what they eat. It is easy to blame executives in the fast food industry for profiting by consumers who choose fast food over fruits and vegetables, but if individuals began to boycott these establishments, healthier foods might begin to appear on the menu. **7**

Consumers have a fatty, unnatural problem served to them on a platter. The average person can no longer see the connection between eating and the land, and the food that consumers are "choosing" to eat is contributing to the obesity epidemic that is clotting up vessels all over America. When consumers unite and demand a better quality product from the food industry, healthier choices will become available. But wouldn't it be pleasant **8** if the executives heading the food industry would make the health of their nation a priority? These executives are people, not machines, and therefore they have no excuse for acting immorally. The corruption present in big corporations is one of capitalism's glaring flaws, and we must work democratically to hold these executives to a higher standard of morality since they refuse to behave well voluntarily.

<u>Works Cited</u> **9**

Berry, Wendell. "The Pleasures of Eating," *What Are People For?* New York: North Point Press, 1990.

Writing to Learn

On the lines below write freely about what you have learned from your examination of this student essay. What did the student do well that you would like to integrate into your own writing? What shortcomings did you identify that you want to remember when examining your draft?

_____

_____

_____

_____

_____

_____

_____

_____

■ Try It

Now that you have analyzed another student's draft, it is time to pick up your own. To bring focus to the process, complete the following statements for your expository essay. Here is a model of how this might look for the expository essay on childhood obesity.

- The purpose of my essay is to *explain the dangers of childhood obesity and the importance of providing young children with a healthy, non-fattening diet.*

- The intended audience for my essay is *anyone with a child or who might someday have children. The essay might also be of interest to people who develop food products for children.*

- I care about this subject because *too many children in this country are overweight and as a result suffer not only from ridicule from their peers but also from health issues that can plague them their whole life.*

- I hope readers will come away from my essay thinking *that it is really important to monitor what children are eating and not to allow them to develop bad eating habits at an early age. Also, I want parents and schools to provide children with healthy and tasty meals and snacks.*

Your Turn

- The purpose of my essay is to _____
  _____
  _____
  _____

- The intended audience for my essay is _____
  _____
  _____
  _____

- I care about this subject because _____
  _____
  _____
  _____

- I hope readers will come away from my essay thinking _____
  _____
  _____
  _____

Turn back to the pages where you drafted your expository essay and apply the same critical skills you used on the sample student essay to your draft. Make notes to yourself about any mistakes you may have made, any areas that need strengthening, or any questions left unanswered for your readers. Rewrite sections that need work.

KNOW IT!

An expository essay achieves its purpose when it explains an issue clearly and coherently, teaching readers about a subject that matters to the writer.

Critically examining other people's writing can help you learn to apply the same critical eye to your own writing. Take any opportunity you get to help a peer critique his or her essay.

LESSON 5 Revising

In a garden you place shrubs and flowers with attention to size, color, and season, carefully considering how each element adds to the cohesiveness of the whole. In the same way writers wrestle with ideas, push words this way and that, take care with sentence structure and word choice, until a cohesive essay emerges. A **cohesive** piece of writing holds together. The separate pieces cling firmly to one another to create the whole.

Readers of expository essays need help seeing where they have been and where they are going. **Transition words and phrases** help hold your essay together by indicating how individual ideas relate to one another. It isn't enough simply to link one point to the next. You want to demonstrate *how* the ideas fit together in your argument. If your essay explains a process that develops over time, you might employ **transitions** like *first, next,* and *finally* to link the steps. If you want to contrast ideas, you might use transitions like *on the other hand, but,* or *nonetheless*. Choosing exactly the right transition will make your essay more accessible, more comprehensible, and more interesting.

Here is a chart of common transitional words and phrases that can help lend cohesion to your writing.

To show time	To contrast	To compare	To add	To clarify	To locate
after	meanwhile	similarly	moreover	for instance	beyond
before	although	just as	in addition	for example	amidst
soon	even so	likewise	along with	in other words	among
meanwhile	yet	accordingly	again	that is	in front of
prior to	as opposed to	in the same way	furthermore	put another way	beside
during	however	also	as well as	to illustrate	over

EXAMPLE

Read the following essay by Charlotte Perkins Gilman, a prominent feminist at the turn of the twentieth century. At the time the essay was written, women wore extremely uncomfortable and complicated dresses much in the way that many women today wear high heels. As you read, underline transitional words and phrases that help you follow Gilman's argument. The first few are marked for you.

Why Women Do Not Reform Their Dress

By Charlotte Perkins Gilman

It would seem <u>at first sight</u> that there was but one answer to this question, <u>namely,</u> that women are fools. When you can plainly prove to a woman that her dress is unhealthful, unbeautiful, immoral, <u>and yet</u> she persists in wearing it, there seems no possible reason but the above. <u>But</u> there is a very simple explanation. A physician complained to me that women came to her actually wearing mechanical appliances to counteract diseases which were caused and fostered by the mechanical weight and pressure of their dress. She could see no reason why a woman should deliberately choose pain and weakness. Here is the reason. Let us take an average woman, with a home, family, and social circle. Like every living organism, she is capable of receiving pain and pleasure. As a human being, she receives these sensations both through mind and body. Now this woman, apart from what she considers duty, will pursue always that course of action which seems to her to bring the most pleasure, or the least pain. This is a law of life, as right and natural as for a plant to grow towards the light. This woman's life as a human being is far more mental than physical; the pleasures and pains of the heart and mind are far more important to her than those of the body. Therefore, if a thing give pain to her body but pleasure to her heart and mind, she will certainly choose it. Let us see now how this question of dress affects mind, heart, and body. The present style of dress means, with varying limits, backache, sideache, headache, and many other ache; corns, lame, tender, or swollen feet, weak clumsy, and useless compared to what they should be; a crowd of diseases, heavy and light; a general condition of feebleness and awkwardness and total inferiority as an animal organism;

with a thousand attendant inconveniences and restrictions and unnatural distortions amounting to hideousness. But it also means the satisfaction of the social conscience; gratification of pride, legitimate and illegitimate; approbation of those loved and admiration of those unknown; satisfaction of a sense of beauty, however false; and a general ease and peace of mind. The true and reasonable dress means perfect ease and health and beauty of body, with the freedom of motion and increase of power and skill resultant therefrom. But it also means long combat with one's own miseducated sense of beauty, and fitness, and with all one's friends' constant disapprobation; ridicule, opposition, an uneasy sense of isolation and disagreeable noticeability, loss of social position, constant mortification and shame. Now, to the average woman, these pains and penalties of the home and social life are infinitely more to be dreaded than the physical ones; and the physical comfort and strength infinitely less to be desired than the mental satisfaction and peace. Physical suffering has been so long considered an integral part of woman's nature, and is still so generally borne, that a little or more or less is no great matter. But to offend and grieve instead of pleasing, to meet opposition and contempt instead of praise and flattery, to change pride for shame,–this is suffering which no woman will accept unless it is proved her duty. And this is why women do not reform their dress.

Try It

Imagine that you were writing an expository essay called "Why Women Wear High Heels." Use transitional words and phrases to link the following sentences into a coherent paragraph. Feel free to rearrange the order of these sentences, combine sentences, or add additional information and your own opinions.

- Shoemakers like Jimmy Choo, Manolo Blahnik, and Christian Louboutin are making a fortune out of women's vanity.
- Women wear high heels in hopes of appearing attractive.
- High heels make a woman look taller.
- High heels make a woman's legs look slimmer.
- Wearing designer heels alters a woman's posture.
- Wearing designer heels changes the way a woman walks.
- Walking in shoes with four- to six-inch heels can permanently damage a woman's feet and legs.
- Podiatrists (foot doctors) report that women who consistently wear high heels often require bunion surgery and corn removal.
- Podiatrists say many women who wear high heels every day experience back and neck pain.
- Fashion magazines feature models wearing shoes no sensible person could walk in for more than a block.
- Women continue to buy and wear designer heels.

Don't limit yourself to the transitional words in the preceding chart. There are many, many more you can use to connect these sentences into a cohesive paragraph. Remember to employ transitions that demonstrate how the two ideas are connected.

For emphasis	To indicate cause and effect	To conclude
in fact,	because	in the end,
even more revealing,	since	finally,
note that	due to	all in all,

Why Women Wear High Heels

_____

_____

_____

_____

_____

_____

_____

_____

_____

_____

_____

_____

_____

_____

_____

_____

_____

Example Paragraph

Shoemakers like Jimmy Choo, Manolo Blahnik, and Christian Louboutin are making a fortune out of women's vanity. Despite the fact that podiatrists report that women who consistently wear high heels complain of back and neck pain and often require bunion surgery and corn removal, women continue to buy and wear designer heels. Why, you ask? The answer is simple. Women ignore the permanent damage they are doing to their feet and legs in order to look taller, slimmer, and sexier. They pursue an illusion, imitating supermodels, and all the while ruin their bodies. Give me flip-flops and tennis shoes any day.

Revising Your Expository Essay

How can you tell if you need to employ more transitions in your writing? Reread your draft, asking yourself the following questions:

1. Does the essay sound choppy?

2. Is it hard to follow the flow from one idea to another?

3. Are there unclear gaps between supporting paragraphs?

You may find that you need to do more than simply insert additional words between sentences. Creating cohesiveness among your points often requires significant rewriting. As you recopy your draft on your own paper or type it on a computer, pause after each sentence to reflect upon whether you have made the connections between ideas within each paragraph and among your paragraphs clear.

Use the following scoring guide to evaluate your draft. Aim to produce an essay that meets all of the expectations for a 5 paper.

EXPOSITORY WRITING RUBRIC (5-point scale)

A 5 expository essay presents a compelling, thorough, and insightful explanation of an issue or process. The writer offers carefully chosen evidence to develop the essay, citing sources and providing commentary and analysis. The essay is focused, demonstrates a clear sense of purpose and audience, and uses appropriate tone and style. Organization is coherent with appropriate transitions between and within paragraphs to create a cohesive whole. Word choice is precise, sentences are varied, and grammatical errors are rare or absent.

A 4 expository essay presents a competent explanation of an issue or process. The writer offers evidence to develop the essay and provides some commentary or analysis of supporting evidence. The essay generally maintains its focus and demonstrates a sense of purpose, tone, and audience. Organization is generally clear with transitions between paragraphs. A competency with language is apparent. Word choice is appropriate and sentences are sometimes varied. Some errors in sentence structure, usage, and mechanics are present.

A 3 expository essay presents a minimally competent explanation of an issue or process. The writer offers some evidence to develop the essay, but the essay lacks commentary and analysis. Some of the evidence may occasionally be inappropriate or weak. The essay generally maintains its focus with minor digressions. Its sense of purpose, tone, and audience may be unclear. Organization is clear enough to follow. A limited control of language is apparent. Word choice is imprecise and sentences may be poorly constructed or confusing. Errors in sentence structure, usage, and mechanics are present.

A 2 expository essay presents a weakly developed explanation of an issue or process. The writer offers minimal and/or inappropriate evidence to support its claim and fails to analyze the evidence offered. The writer's ideas are difficult to follow because of significant problems in one or more of the following areas: unclear focus, lack of organization, weak controlling idea, and redundancy. Style and tone may be inappropriate for the audience. Writing demonstrates weak control of language. A pattern of errors in grammar, usage, and mechanics significantly interferes with meaning.

A 1 expository essay presents an ineffective explanation of an issue or process. Ideas and explanations are absent, irrelevant, unsupported by evidence, or incomprehensible. The essay demonstrates significant problems that make the writer's ideas difficult to follow and lacks focus and organization. Style and tone are inappropriate for the audience. Writing demonstrates poor control of language. Errors in grammar, usage, and mechanics are pervasive and obstruct meaning.

Writing a Compelling Opening

You may have noticed as you read the scoring guide for expository essays that one of the features that separates a 4-essay from a 5-essay is that the better essay is "compelling." But what does it mean for an essay to be compelling? Compelling writing arouses strong interest and demands a reader's attention. How can you make your draft more compelling? Much depends upon your first sentences. Like a fisherman attaching a lure to his hook, you want readers to bite.

Take a look at the following opening sentence from the essay, "Taking the Fight Out of Teenagers." The author uses **rhetorical questions** to lure readers into her essay by arousing interest in the subject. As you instinctively begin imagining your answers to these questions, you find yourself drawn into the argument. Gotcha!

From "Taking the Fight Out of Teenagers"

> The recent spate of disturbances on high school campuses across the city is just that—disturbing. What are all these teenagers fighting about? Why are they so angry? How is it that teenagers' fuses are so short?

Write a rhetorical question or two that might help to make your essay introduction more compelling.

_____

_____

_____

_____

_____

Consider other ways to make the opening of your expository essay more compelling. You might:

- tell an illustrative anecdote.

- present a startling statistic.

- begin with a dramatic quotation.

KNOW IT!

Transitions guide readers through your essay by helping them understand how the ideas are logically connected.

It is important to start your essay with a "hook"—something that will catch your readers' attention and drive them to keep reading.

LESSON **6** Editing

The word *plagiarism* comes from the Latin word *plagiarius*, meaning "kidnapper." It was first used to refer to a literary thief by the Roman poet Martial. Presenting the words or ideas of others as though they are your own is a kind of kidnapping, one that you never want to be guilty of.

Information ready to cut and paste into expository essays is so readily available on the Internet that plagiarism can be a great temptation. To ensure the originality of student work, many college instructors have students turn their papers in to software programs that automatically check thousands of sources. The easiest way to avoid falling into the trap of plagiarism is to **cite** all your sources with care. Both direct quotations and the *ideas* of others must be attributed to their original sources—in other words, you have to give credit to, or tell, where the words or ideas came from.

There are three authoritative formats or editorial style guidelines for citing sources.

1. **MLA (Modern Language Association)** style guidelines are used mainly in English and language courses. http://www.mla.org/style

2. **APA (American Psychological Association)** style guidelines are used mainly by social and physical sciences. http://apastyle.apa.org/

3. **CMS (Chicago Manual of Style)** guidelines are used mainly in publishing, history, and related fields. http://www.chicagomanualofstyle.org/home.html

When turning in an essay, make sure you know which format your teacher expects you to use. There is no need to memorize all the rules for citing sources using the various style guidelines. Just know where to go to find the guidelines you are required to use. The examples used in this lesson follow MLA guidelines.

For a complete guide to MLA citations, see p. 227.

EXAMPLE

Without careful citation you run the risk of plagiarism. Reference to authoritative sources also helps strengthen your argument by showing the reader how well researched your essay is. The following is a list of basics to remember when citing sources.

- When referring to the words or ideas of others within your essay, place the author's name and the page number where you found the information inside parenthesis at the end of the sentence.

- The period should be placed after the parenthesis.

- Do not put a comma between the name and the page number.

- If you use the name of the person you are citing in your sentence, include only the page number and do not repeat the name within the parenthesis.

- If your source is a Web site:

  - include the author if known.

  - If no name is associated with the material, use the first word of the title of the article.

  - The URL address should appear only on your **Works Cited page**.

- Every citation within your essay should correspond with an entry on your Works Cited page.

Example for a quotation

"Many overweight children are in danger of developing Type 2 diabetes" (Johnston 87).

Example for a paraphrase of another person's ideas

According to Dr. Seth Johnston, children who weigh more than normal for their age run the risk of developing childhood diabetes (87).

Example for a quotation from a Web site

Notice that the URL address <http://www.heavyteen/diabetes.html> should appear only on your Works Cited page, not within the text of your essay.

"Type 2 diabetes can be prevented. If overweight children simply exercised more and lost some of their excess weight, the disease would be far less prevalent" (Taylor, par. 8)

Formatting Your Quotations

- If you want to include a quotation that is more than four lines long, start the quotation on a new line and indent one inch from the left margin. When using MLA guidelines the block of quoted text should continue to be double spaced along with the rest of your essay. Known as a block quote, this type of quote does not need quotation marks, even if it is word for word.

- Try to avoid repeating the "he said" or "she said" pattern when quoting from sources. The following alternatives will help lend variety to your essay.

comments	claims	predicts
argues	states	proposes
observes	insists	notes

[TIP]

You do not need to cite sources for proverbs or sayings, common knowledge, or well-known facts.

[TIP]

Use good judgment when deciding how much of a quotation to include in your essay. Sometimes less is more.

- Sometimes you may wish to quote only a portion of a passage. If you choose to leave out words from the original quotation, insert an ellipsis (. . .) for the omitted portion of the quote. Be careful not to alter the original meaning of the quotation.

  - Dr. Johnston worries that, "Too many children are being put at risk for Type 2 diabetes as a result of poor eating habits . . . resulting in long-term health problems" (75).

- Integrating portions of quotations into your own sentences can help your essay flow more smoothly and sound less like a collection of researched facts. For example you might write:

  - According to Dr. Johnston, parents "should monitor children's food intake," and at the same time "provide them with healthy alternatives to fast food" (92).

Creating a Works Cited page

A works cited page should include all the sources that you quoted or cited within the essay. Every citation within your essay should be accompanied by an entry on a works cited page; however, multiple quotes from a single source only need one entry.

- Label the page "Works Cited" and center the title, but do not underline or put quotation marks around it.

- Double-space all citations. Do not skip extra lines between citations.

- Use a hanging indent for entries. The first line of each entry should be flush with the left margin. Any subsequent lines should be indented.

- List entries alphabetically, listing the author's last name first.

- Alphabetize works with no author by the first major word of their titles.

For books, citations should read:

Author's last name, First name. *Title of book*. Place of publication: Publisher, Year of publication.

- Gilmore, Tony. *Childhood Obesity: Why It Happens and How to Prevent It*. New York: Dover Press, 2005.

For journals, magazines, and newspapers, citations should read:

Author's last name, First name. "Title of article." *Title of Periodical* Day, Month, Year: pages.

- Crawford, Susan. "Time to Eat and Time to Play." *Parents' Magazine* Mar. 2007: 89–92.

[TIP]

When creating entries for a works cited page, pay close attention to the formatting and punctuation guidelines for that type of entry. The rules are strict and must be followed closely.

For electronic sources:

Include as much information as available. Common identifying features you should try to locate somewhere on the site include:

- The name of the author or editor of the Web site (if available)

- The title of the individual page or article you are citing

- The name of the Web site

- Date of posting or last update of the Web site

- Date you accessed the material

- Electronic address, URL printed between carets < >

In MLA style, the *W* in "Web site" is capitalized and *Web site* is written as two words.

Battle, Judy Shepps. "Diabetes and Kids." *Overweight Teen.* 2004.
January 2, 2009. <http://www.overweightteen.com/diabetes-kids.html>.

■ Try It

1. Edit your expository essay, making sure that all your sources are cited correctly.

2. Following the MLA guidelines offered in this lesson and on pages 227–230, use this chart to help you create a Works Cited page for your expository essay.

Author's name	Title of work	Place of Publication	Publisher	Date of publication
1.				
2.				
3.				
4.				

Proofreading Your Paper

Along with the editing guidelines provided in this lesson for citing sources and for your Works Cited page, you also need to **proofread** your expository essay for mechanical errors. One way to catch careless errors like missing words is to read your essay out loud. Another is to read your essay from the bottom up, starting with your final sentence and working your way backwards to the top of the page. This odd exercise helps you catch errors by paying close attention to every individual word and punctuation mark.

Use this checklist to help you proofread your paper before turning it in.

For more information on these grammar topics, see pp. 218–226.

Ask yourself:	If necessary, make these changes:
Does every sentence begin with a capital letter? Are all proper nouns capitalized?	Insert capital letters where needed. Eliminate unnecessary or random capital letters.
Is every sentence complete?	Add a subject or verb to make the fragment a complete sentence.
Are any of your longer sentences run-ons?	Punctuate the sentence to correct the run-on or divide the sentence into shorter complete sentences.
Have you used verb tenses consistently?	Revise verb forms to establish consistency in tenses and avoid jumping from past to present tense without reason.
Are pronoun references clear?	Check and correct any pronouns that do not agree with their antecedents in number or gender.
Is every word in the essay spelled correctly?	Use spell-check and a dictionary to ensure that your spelling is perfect.

KNOW IT! It is critical that you give credit to the source of your research and ideas, even if you are not quoting a source directly. Plagiarism is a serious offense and the punishment can be severe. Be sure to follow the style rules—most likely MLA—when citing sources within your paper and when creating your Works Cited page. You can lose many unnecessary points by not following the format correctly!

Wrap It Up

Use the rubric below (introduced in lesson 2.5) to evaluate your essay before handing it in.

EXPOSITORY WRITING RUBRIC (5-point scale)

A 5 expository essay presents a compelling, thorough, and insightful explanation of an issue or process. The writer offers carefully chosen evidence to develop the essay, citing sources and providing commentary and analysis. The essay is focused, demonstrates a clear sense of purpose and audience, and uses appropriate tone and style. Organization is coherent with appropriate transitions between and within paragraphs to create a cohesive whole. Word choice is precise, sentences are varied, and grammatical errors are rare or absent.

A 4 expository essay presents a competent explanation of an issue or process. The writer offers evidence to develop the essay and provides some commentary or analysis of supporting evidence. The essay generally maintains its focus and demonstrates a sense of purpose, tone, and audience. Organization is generally clear with transitions between paragraphs. A competency with language is apparent. Word choice is appropriate and sentences are sometimes varied. Some errors in sentence structure, usage, and mechanics are present.

A 3 expository essay presents a minimally competent explanation of an issue or process. The writer offers some evidence to develop the essay, but the essay lacks commentary and analysis. Some of the evidence may occasionally be inappropriate or weak. The essay generally maintains its focus with minor digressions. Its sense of purpose, tone, and audience may be unclear. Organization is clear enough to follow. A limited control of language is apparent. Word choice is imprecise and sentences may be poorly constructed or confusing. Errors in sentence structure, usage, and mechanics are present.

A 2 expository essay presents a weakly developed explanation of an issue or process. The writer offers minimal and/or inappropriate evidence to support its claim and fails to analyze the evidence offered. The writer's ideas are difficult to follow because of significant problems in one or more of the following areas: unclear focus, lack of organization, weak controlling idea, and redundancy. Style and tone may be inappropriate for the audience. Writing demonstrates weak control of language. A pattern of errors in grammar, usage, and mechanics significantly interferes with meaning.

A 1 expository essay presents an ineffective explanation of an issue or process. Ideas and explanations are absent, irrelevant, unsupported by evidence, or incomprehensible. The essay demonstrates significant problems that make the writer's ideas difficult to follow and lacks focus and organization. Style and tone are inappropriate for the audience. Writing demonstrates poor control of language. Errors in grammar, usage, and mechanics are pervasive and obstruct meaning.

My paper should score a: _____

Before moving on to the next unit, take 15 minutes or so to reflect upon what you have learned about writing expository essays. On the lines below discuss how the process worked for you.

What do you feel are your essay's greatest strengths? _____
_____
_____
_____
_____
_____

Where do you see weaknesses? _____
_____
_____
_____
_____
_____

What advice would you offer to a friend who was about to begin this unit on expository writing?
_____
_____
_____
_____
_____
_____

Are you happy with your finished product? _____
_____
_____
_____
_____
_____

What might you do differently the next time you write an expository essay? _____
_____
_____
_____
_____

UNIT 3 Writing to Reflect

LESSON **1** Prewriting

Y ou know how to tell stories about odd things that happen to you. You do it all the time with friends. **Reflective writing** takes this natural process one step further by asking you to tell a story about something that happened to you and then explore the event's significance. Why does it matter? What does it all mean? What have you learned from your experience?

Reflective writing is more common than you might have realized. Magazines often carry reflective essays by writers who have a gift for taking what occurs in their own lives and finding universal themes within everyday events. Sometimes writers present their reflection as lessons learned. Sometimes they simply raise questions about what it means to be human. Personal statements for college applications are another form of reflective essay. Admissions officers want to know more than simply what has happened to you in your life. They want to know how these events have shaped you as a person. Individuals training to work in the health professions are often asked to write reflectively about what they observe happening with patients. The idea behind this practice is to help future doctors, nurses, and technicians learn from a medical event by analyzing it. The lessons learned from one patient can then be applied to the treatment of future patients.

> [TIP]
>
> When composing a reflective essay, many writers do not always know exactly what they have to say about an incident before they begin to write. This kind of writing is often an act of discovery.

When you write to reflect, you take a step back from events and consider their implications. What does this **autobiographical incident** say about you? What does it suggest about others or about the world? Though reflective writing tells a story, it is more than straightforward **narration**. Though reflective writing may contain descriptive elements, it is more than simple description. It may try to convince readers of something, but it is not primarily persuasive. Though writing reflectively may help you begin to understand things that have happened to you, it is not merely an explanation or report. A reflective essay is an account of something that has happened to you *and* an analysis of how the incident made you feel and think.

Reflective writing begins with a description of an experience or incident. The writer then analyzes or interprets that experience, closing with a discussion of how the experience affected him or her. When reflecting on an autobiographical incident, you turn your memory of events over and over in your mind, examining them from various perspectives and contemplating the possibilities for learning from the memory.

<u>EXAMPLE</u>

Read the following reflective essay by a mother whose son got her banned from AOL. The writer describes an occurrence from her own life and reflects upon its significance. As you read, ask yourself, "Is this essay about her son getting in trouble or is it about something else as well?" To help you answer this question, read with a pen or pencil in hand, marking narrative details (events that occurred to the writer and her son) with an *N* in the margin and reflective **commentary** (the writer's comments on events) with a *C*.

Kicked Offline

When the message "invalid user" first appeared on my screen, I wasn't much concerned. This had to be some mistake, a glitch. Having navigated America Online® Service for some months, I was pretty sure of myself electronically. I got up to dial their 800 number without the slightest trepidation. Along the way I was intercepted by my 13-year-old son. "Oh, Mom, I forgot to tell you, I already called and they said they need to talk to you."

This was not a good sign. When I reached an operator, I was informed that our AOL® Service account had been terminated. "But why? This can't be. I go on-line 20 times a day. I have cards and stationery with my email address imprinted. How can I reinstate it?" The operator informed me that someone had been caught (I had a very clear idea who) going into rooms online and downloading copyrighted software. My pleas that this was a kid messing around fell on deaf ears. Our only recourse was to write a letter of appeal to a group called the Community Action Team. "Write a letter? I need to pick up my mail now!" Too bad. The fastest I could get to CAT was by fax. No phone number available.

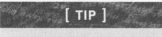

[TIP]

CAT refers to the Community Action Team.

Fuming, I set upon my child, railing at him for all the trouble this was causing me. I screamed that his pranks were interfering with my work. James argued that he hadn't done anything wrong, that he didn't even want the stuff he was downloading. His friends at school had told him about the online chat room and he just wanted to see if it worked. "Do you really think I care about an upgraded version of Microsoft Word?" I told him he was grounded for life and sat down to write the appeal letter. I arrogantly assumed that groveling and abject apologies would be accepted as proof of James' sincerity never to do it again and my ability to enforce this. I was wrong.

The next day the Community Action Team rejected my appeal, and I was officially expelled from the America Online Community forever. Stunned, I could only set to work establishing another Internet hookup and hope that none of the lost messages had been vital. I had 200 change of address notices to send. Toiling away at my keyboard, a light seemed to dawn. AOL® was right. My son and I really didn't get it about intellectual property rights. What I saw as annoying mischief was serious infringement on the rights of software developers. James and his buddies were thieves. Guilty, I stopped entering data for a heart-to-heart with James.

"Do you know that what you were doing on-line is just like stealing from a store?"

"No way, Mom. We were just fooling around."

"Yes, way. You were fooling with things people pay money for. You were taking it for nothing."

"But we didn't even use the stuff."

"Tell that to a judge. Are your friends still going in those rooms?"

"Naw, they got kicked off too."

It turns out that America Online®, citing breach of contract, pulled the plug on thousands of users that month. James and his friends' attitude toward online rules was epidemic. So was my casual response to what he had done. Though furious, my anger had been over the discomfort he caused me. I don't think for a minute that I would have responded in such a cavalier manner had James been caught shoplifting. If I'm honest, a part of me was secretly proud of having such a clever son. Both parent and child needed a wake-up call.

I thought about calling James' middle school and demanding they include lessons on computer ethics and electronic etiquette in every keyboarding and computer class. Children need to be taught about intellectual property rights as well as warned of the repercussions of flaunting copyright. But schools will never be able to respond as quickly as this problem demands. Nor will they be able to handle it alone. Do you know what your child is doing online? Save yourself humiliation and the expense of new stationery. Find out.

On the chart below, copy passages from the essay that you marked as narrative details (*N*) and reflective commentary (*C*).

Narrative details	Reflective commentary

Use the following questions to help you analyze what makes "Kicked Offline" such a powerful reflective essay.

1. How does opening with a description of a problem make you want to read on?

_____

_____

_____

_____

2. What can you infer about the writer's relationship with her son from the way she talks with him? What does the parenthetical expression "(I had a very clear idea who)" suggest about her thoughts and feelings towards her child?

_____

_____

_____

_____

3. How did the conversational tone of this essay affect you as a reader?

_____

_____

_____

_____

4. Do you agree with the writer that, "Children need to be taught about intellectual property rights as well as warned of the repercussions of flaunting copyright"? How does the author support this statement?

_____

_____

_____

_____

5. What has the writer learned from reflecting on her experience of getting kicked offline?

_____

_____

_____

_____

■ Try It

To help you choose an autobiographical incident worth writing about, use this **cluster** to brainstorm ideas that might work as the seeds of a reflective essay. Write down puzzling or disturbing events, irritating moments, delightful occurrences, and important changes in your life. Include small as well as large events—the time you got lost, a trip to the emergency room, scoring a goal, the death of a goldfish, eating your first oyster. The trick to creating a useful cluster is to let one idea lead you to the next. Don't say "no" to any memory that presents itself. Just jot it down in another circle. The first few circles have been drawn for you. As you brainstorm, add more circles and clusters as necessary.

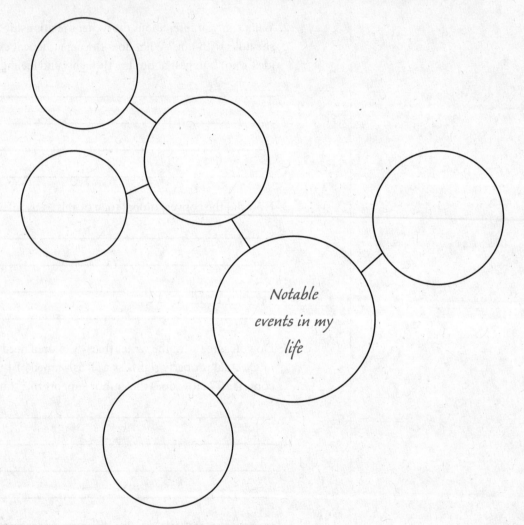

Now choose one of these incidents to describe in detail. The kind of incident that will work best for a reflective essay is one that had a powerful effect upon you, something you think back on often, an occurrence that for some reason has stayed with you. It can be funny or somber, tragic or uplifting. It should lend itself to detailed sensory descriptions; this will make it easier for the reader to connect with the story.

On the lines below write for 15 minutes about what happened. Be sure to include information that tells your readers the important details about the event: who, what, where and when. If you had a photograph of the incident, what would be in it? Remember that you are trying to paint this picture in words.

[TIP]

To get your storytelling juices flowing, it can help to tell your story to a friend. Find someone willing to listen and recount the events you plan to write about. Pay attention to any questions your listener may have and be sure to include these details in your description.

_____

_____

_____

_____

_____

_____

_____

_____

_____

_____

_____

_____

_____

_____

_____

_____

_____

_____

_____

_____

_____

KNOW IT! An autobiographical incident is an event in a person's life that had an effect on that person. The event may have shaped the person's character or future behavior.

LESSON 2 Taking a Reflective Stance

When writing a reflective essay, it is easy to get caught up in the telling of your autobiographical incident and shortchange the reflection. You probably found it relatively easy to tell a story about something that happened. The challenge now is to use the event as a springboard for exploring the significance of your experience. Remember to keep asking yourself, "So what? Why does this matter?"

Reflective writing is highly personal. It includes doubts, anxieties, or worries that the events may have inspired in the writer. In "Kicked Offline," the author describes the trouble she experienced as a result of her son's illegal downloading of software and then comments on how this experience caused her to rethink her attitude towards intellectual property rights as well as her attitude about supervising what her son was doing online. Such commentary is what distinguishes reflective writing from simple narration. Reflective writing includes both the story and how the writer feels about the story. Readers learn not only what happened but also how what happened affected the writer.

Reflective writing engages the reader in the story and then proceeds to convey a larger message. Events seem to unfold right before your eyes. You experience them along with the narrator. When the teenage son in "Kicked Offline" says that he "forgot" to tell his mom about the problem, we have a feeling he is hiding something. When the mother yells at him about the trouble he is causing, we sense that she is mad for the wrong reason. The essay walks reader through the development of the writer's thinking. Reflection causes the writer to revise her initial response to events and begin to explore what she learned from them. At the end of the essay, she offers advice to others based upon this reflection and learning. While reflection sometimes results in new insights, at other times it raises new questions that remain—at least for the time being—unanswered.

EXAMPLE

Read the following reflective essay and use the graphic organizer to help you examine the essay with the eyes of a writer.

Showered in Sewage

A few months ago my best friend and I were out on our usual jog through the neighborhood. It was a beautiful summer day. As we crossed the street in front of a large yellow truck, cheerfully chatting about this and that, a sanitation worker accidentally dropped the high-pressure hose he was holding in his hands. Before the man could bring what seemed like a massive live snake back under control, the two of us were sprayed from head to toe in raw sewage. Twice.

Needless to say it was a nasty business. We ran back to my friend's house, showered under the hottest water we could stand, and dumped the clothes

[TIP]

Notice how writers of reflective essays use **personal pronouns** like "I" and "we" freely and often employ a conversational tone.

we were wearing into the trash. As soon as we were dry and wrapped in bathrobes, we sat down to write.

Together we composed a complaint to the Los Angeles Sanitation Department. We didn't threaten to sue the city or in any way suggest that the man with the hose was at fault. It was an accident. We explained that though the incident was truly unpleasant, it had not resulted in any lasting physical harm or injury. What we did claim was that the city owed us for our discarded clothes.

Now the cost of two T-shirts and two pairs of shorts is a small thing, but writing that letter helped us feel a lot better. Setting out our complaint on paper got the bad taste out of our mouths—yes, the water from the hose got into our mouths along with in our eyes and ears—and allowed us to begin to laugh about it all.

When our $30 checks from the Sanitation Department arrived in the mail, we cheered. This time around, the pen was mightier than the hose.

Question	Response
What personal experience is described in this essay?	
What details most helped to create a vivid picture of the experience? Why?	
What seems to be the writer's attitude towards this experience?	
What did the writer learn from this experience? What made it significant?	

Try It

The following list of questions can help you begin to think reflectively about the incident you described in Lesson 1. Answer each question on the lines that follow.

1. What does this incident reveal about me?

_____

_____

_____

_____

_____

2. What is there about this experience that continues to bother or puzzle me?

_____

_____

_____

_____

_____

3. Were there previous similar incidents or have there been subsequent similar incidents? What do the incidents have in common?

_____

_____

_____

_____

_____

4. Why do these events stick out in my mind?

_____

_____

_____

_____

_____

[TIP]

Though these questions are numbered, don't think of this list as a series of steps. Reflection is often a somewhat haphazard process with new insights appearing when you least expect them.

5. How did I feel about what happened when the incident occurred? How do I feel about it now?

_____

_____

_____

_____

_____

6. If I step back from the experience, does it seem different?

_____

_____

_____

_____

_____

7. Have I learned anything from this experience? Why or why not?

_____

_____

_____

_____

_____

8. Will what I learned affect my future actions? Has it or will it change me in some way?

_____

_____

_____

_____

_____

9. Are there broader moral or ethical implications to this incident?

_____

_____

_____

_____

_____

10. What is the significance of this incident?

_____

_____

_____

_____

_____

A Different Perspective

Another way to help you reflect objectively upon your autobiographical incident is to imagine the events from a different perspective. Choose one of the two activities below and then answer the questions on the lines that follow.

Activity #1: Fictionalize It

Imagine that these events happened to someone else, possibly a fictional character in a novel or film. Jot down notes about the incident and about the significant themes your novel or movie will explore, including key dramatic moments and important themes about life and human nature.

_____

_____

_____

_____

_____

_____

_____

Activity #2: Another Point of View

Consider how your autobiographical incident might appear to:

- an authority figure such as a police officer, doctor, or parent.

- a loyal friend who cares about your welfare and has your best interest at heart.

- a disinterested bystander who may have observed what happens but has no interest or stake in the matter.

- an antagonist or enemy who does not want you to succeed.

Jot down any observations you have about how others might have perceived the events described in your autobiographical incident.

_____

_____

_____

_____

_____

_____

_____

_____

_____

Looking at the event through another person's eyes can help you be more objective about what happened. It may also trigger additional reflection on the significance of the incident.

 **KNOW IT!** Reflection entails more than a simple description of events. You must examine events with an eye for larger significance and meaning.

 Before moving ahead to the drafting lesson, pause to consider whether the incident you have chosen will work well for your reflective essay. Not every story is good material for a reflective essay. If you think you need to start over with a new experience, consider:

- An experience in which you were taught a sport or other physical skill such as riding a bicycle or skateboarding. Did you listen to advice from others? Did you have to learn the hard way? What larger lessons did you learn in the process? What questions do you still have about the experience?
- An experience that has led you toward a decision about your future career. What happened that made you want to move in a particular direction in your life? Was there a particular individual who influenced you by his or her example? Did someone else's service to you make you want to serve others in this way?
- An experience in school or on the job that was memorable either for its pleasure or for its pain. What caused this event to stick with you over the years? How did it shape you as a student or employee? How did it influence your attitude toward your school or your job?
- An experience that brought home to you the importance of your family's ethnic culture. Why is this tradition or practice important to you? Did you always feel as you do? How will you help to keep this tradition alive?

Remember how you learned to ride a bike? Someone held the handlebars with one hand and your wobbly seat with the other. Urging you to pedal, this trusty helper showered you with encouragement. "Good job! A little faster now. You can do it. Keep going. Good. You've got it!" The guidelines that follow provide similar support for drafting your reflective essay.

Though the possibilities for shaping a reflective essay are many, the first time you try your hand at this kind of essay it may be best to work within a familiar organizational structure.

The introduction of your reflective essay should engage readers in the story you are about to tell and make them want to know more about how the events affected you. You might start with the **inciting incident**, or the first moment of conflict within your story. It might also be important to describe the **setting**. Was it a dark and stormy night or a beautiful spring morning? Was rain pouring down from the sky or did the sun's rays sparkle off your car windows? Details about the time, the weather, and your surroundings can help to set the mood and provide additional clues to the significance of the events.

Reflective essays rarely state their thesis up front but may include a hint at the significance of the experience in the opening paragraph. There are various ways you can choose to drop this hint. Sometimes you may want to offer a clue. Other times the tone of voice you use to open your essay sets the mood for the insight you will later draw from these events.

The body of your essay is your autobiographical incident. Try to tell your story as simply and clearly as possible. Most reflective essays are told in **chronological order**, or the order in which the events actually occurred.

The conclusion of your reflective essay should focus on the significance of the events described. Include a discussion of why the incident was significant for you and also how it might be significant for readers. What insights about human nature or the world can be drawn from this story?

As you draft your essay, you will want to include details that make the events come to life for readers. Consider including dialogue in the course of your storytelling. Let your characters speak for themselves. You can use dialogue to advance the action in your story. You probably don't remember exactly what people said when the incident occurred, but try to duplicate the kind of speech that was used at the time. Each time the speaker changes, remember to start a new paragraph.

EXAMPLE

Take a look at what this organizational structure would have looked like for the short, light-hearted reflective essay "Showered in Sewage" from Lesson 2.

Introduction	**Attention-getter:** "Showered in Sewage" title
	Background: one day in the life of friends who jog together regularly
	Hint: The tone is cheerful while describing a disgusting experience.
Body	**Inciting incident:** A sanitation worker drops his hose, showering the joggers with sewage.
	What happened next: Joggers return home, shower, and throw away their clothes.
	Final moment: The two friends write a letter of complaint to the Department of Sanitation.
Conclusion	**Significance of the experience:** Writing the letter of complaint helped the joggers deal with the accident and get over it more quickly.
	Insight: Next time something bad happens, put the complaint in writing. It's possible you'll be compensated.

Try It

Use this graphic organizer to help you plan your reflective essay.

Introduction	**Attention-getter:**
	Background:
	Hint:
Body	**Inciting incident:**
	What happened next:
	Final moment:
Conclusion	**Significance of the experience:**
	Insight:

With your plan in place, drafting your reflective essay should be relatively easy. Write freely with the knowledge that you can revise later. Imagine that you are telling a story to a friend. Relax into the writing. Just keep pedaling! Keep pedaling and your sense of how it feels to get it right on paper will develop. Keep pedaling and you will inevitably find yourself picking up speed. Keep pedaling and though you may come across rough spots on the road and even take a few spills, the ride is worth it.

_____

_____

_____

_____

_____

_____

_____

_____

_____

_____

_____

_____

_____

_____

_____

_____

_____

_____

_____

_____

_____

_____

[TIP]

It is easier to trim and tighten a long story during revision than to add to the story later.

_____

_____

_____

_____

_____

_____

_____

_____

_____

_____

_____

KNOW IT! When retelling an autobiographical incident, be sure to include who was there, where the events occurred, and what you heard, saw, smelled, and felt. Describe the scene so that readers will feel they were there.

Use the following checklist to determine if your draft is ready for revision. If you check "No, Needs Work" for any of the criteria, go back and work some more on your draft. Remember that most writers draft many times before creating something they are satisfied with enough to move on to revising and editing.

My reflective essay draft:	Yes	No, Needs Work
• describes an incident using concrete detail, sensory images, and clear narration		
• presents a natural progression of ideas		
• analyzes my experience		
• offers insight into the world around me		

The writing in my draft:	Yes	No, Needs Work
• is exploratory, raising questions I may or may not have answers to		
• makes connections between my experiences and the larger world		
• reveals my thoughts and feelings		
• avoids being "preachy"		

LESSON 4 Examining a Model Reflective Essay

What makes a story come to life for a reader? You want your audience to feel as though they were there with you. How do you make this happen on the page? Try to show, rather than tell, readers what you saw, heard, smelled, and felt. The trick behind "showing" is to appeal to your readers' senses.

Simply telling your readers how you felt when something happened isn't enough. You need to animate the scene and show them how you behaved and reacted. If you cried, let them see and taste the tears. If you laughed, let them hear the sound of your deep chuckle or your high-pitched squeal. If you ate a rotten tomato, let them feel the awful squish in your hands and taste the mold.

Imagine if the author of "Showered in Sewage" (pages 96–97) had simply told you that she once got a refund from the sanitation department. Would you have cared? As an experienced writer, the author knew that she had to make the experience of being showered in sewage come alive for her readers. She painted a picture of herself and her friend on a walk, and then instead of telling you that the day went wrong, she showed you what happened:

- "a sanitation worker accidentally dropped the high-pressure hose he was holding in his hands"

- "what seemed like a massive live snake"

- "sprayed from head to toe in raw sewage. Twice."

The author offers these details and others, like "dumped the clothes we were wearing into the trash," to help readers share in the experience. By not drawing conclusions for you, the author engages you more fully in the story. This is the kind of lively storytelling that will make your autobiographical incident matter to readers and ultimately make your reflective commentary more insightful.

EXAMPLE

Here is a reflective essay written by a student who was born in Pakistan and came to the United States when she was twelve. Read about her reflections on the neighborhood of her childhood, underlining places where you feel she has done a particularly good job of showing rather than telling. Put a squiggly line under sentences where you feel she lapses into telling and where more concrete description would improve the essay.

[TIP]

"Showing" isn't simply a matter of layering more adjectives onto your sentences. It is the combination of concrete details and action that allow a reader to see what you saw and feel what you felt.

Reflecting on a Box

Thinking about my future makes me think about my past. It makes me think. Who am I? What am I? What is the purpose of my life? The other day I found an old box, a box which carried no meaning to the world, but carried all the answers for me. A box, which contained my history, my past and the key to my future.

Who am I? As I think back about two years, it takes me to a place different from here where happiness prevails, love exists and respect is being preached and carried out. A place where the old are wise and not a burden. I hear the birds chirping. I see the first of the sun's rays trying to find its way through the clouds to shine on the windows of the houses; to shine on the roads; to shine over the horizon; to announce the beginning of a new day. I see it, very vaguely, but I see it.

The neighborhood was compact, the streets were small and the houses were bricked together. I knew the name of my next door neighbor and the one next to him, and they knew me and were part of my life. They shared sorrows with me and spread happiness throughout the land and made it an ever so beautiful place. It was a land full of emotions. A home for love where the hearts of the people living in the houses were welded together with the love they shared, not by how much was in their pockets. It was not only a home full of love, but it was a community of love, brought together under the closed and narrow streets and the local gossip. A community under the love that was showered and under the burdens that were shared. No need to call 911; I had my neighbors. My friends were my mentors, my parents were always there for me, and my grandma held the keys to the treasures of endless story time.

Waking up by the sound of the rooster, hearing the holy call from the mosque, smelling the pure air and feeling the coolness in that warm morning wind reminds me of the beginning of a day. The day rolled on as more of the sun's light found its way out. Families got up, made their beds, and welcomed the new morning with joy, a new hope, and a smile on their face.

The scene was more relaxed, there was no rush, as the whole family came to the dining table to eat breakfast and share their plans for the day. The house was soon empty as the school bell rang and as the husbands went to work. The day was soon over as the sun's rays were not strong enough to fight the powerful darkness of the skies. The family returned home and washed themselves before heading off to the nightly religious school. This is where I learned about my religion, where I socialized with my fellow friends and made new ones. A place that was not only my second home but also a home for all the community's kids to enjoy and relax.

The lighted streets turned dark, gloomy and scary as the city officials announced the nightly power cut from nine to eleven. They called it power saving, we called it fun time. The streetlights were out but the streets were all lit up as we played hide-and-go-seek in the dark, flashing our mini-torches trying to find the other kids. Neighbors walking and discussing their lives, men sitting out on the grass playing cards, children running around in circles with their moms trying to catch them and the dads watching and laughing out loud. It was indeed leisure time. We didn't care about work, what time we had to be up the next morning or about the world around us. All we cared about was having fun. Everyone had something to do. The old ladies discussed new ways of making delicious meals with their secret herbs and spices. Dads discussed what was wrong with the political leaders. The moms talked about the rising prices at the grocery store and the kids ran around reminding them of their childhood. With so much love in a community, surely the world was very small and beautiful.

The community that spread across only four blocks, that came together for the purpose of religion, and stayed together because of their love gave me memories that will last a lifetime. I see it completely now and I miss it. I miss the closeness of my whole family, their love and the fun times I have spent with them. I miss the easy, relaxed days, the simple lifestyle and the idea of a network of families. I miss it all but will treasure it forever.

On the lines below, take three examples where the author lapsed into telling, not showing. Rewrite them, adding concrete **sensory details** to strengthen the description.

- **Original phrase/sentence #1:** _____

_____

_____

Revised description: _____

_____

_____

_____

_____

- **Original phrase/sentence #2:** _____

_____

_____

Revised description: _____

_____

_____

_____

- **Original phrase/sentence #3:** _____

_____

_____

Revised description: _____

_____

_____

_____

_____

Focus on Verbs

As you work to show rather than tell in your writing, pay attention to the verbs you use. Inexperienced writers often overuse abstract verbs like *go* and *get*. More specific and concrete verbs convey the action both more clearly and more concisely. It could take an extra sentence to explain how a character ran when substituting *bolted* for *ran* gets the job done in a single word. Notice how the concrete verbs are not necessarily longer or more obscure words. They are simply more precise.

Abstract (telling) verb	get	go
More specific verbs	buy	fly
	acquire	drive
	borrow	swim
	steal	run
Concrete (showing) verbs	For "steal"	For "run"
	burglarize	dash
	embezzle	bound
	swipe	scamper
	swindle	dart
	rip off	rush

A thesaurus can be very helpful as you strive to make your word choice more precise. If you are working on a computer, most word processing programs have a built-in thesaurus on the Tools menu. You can find an online thesaurus at www.thesaurus.com or at www.merriam-webster.com. Be careful when you select what you believe is a more precise word from a thesaurus listing; make certain that you know the word's full meaning and connotations. You don't want to write *scamper* when you really mean *bound!*

Try It

[TIP]

When writing about a painful memory, don't tell readers about how you were upset; show them your clenched teeth, let them see the beads of sweat on your brow, let them feel your knees wobbling!

For practice, try to think of four more precise, concrete verbs to substitute for these abstract verbs. If you run out of ideas, use a thesaurus.

Abstract Verbs	Concrete Verbs
eat	1. 2. 3. 4.
hit	1. 2. 3. 4.
touch	1. 2. 3. 4.
walk	1. 2. 3. 4.

Appealing to the Senses

As any advertiser knows, the best way to attract interest in a product is to appeal to the consumer's senses. Thumb through any magazine to see how the words and images on the page attempt to stimulate your senses and make you equate pleasure with their product. The same is true in descriptive writing. In your description of an autobiographical incident, use language that stimulates readers' sensory memories, for example of smelly old dogs they have known or juicy fresh strawberries smothered in cream. The most common sensory images appeal to sight, smell, taste, touch, and sound.

Choose one moment from the events you described in your reflective essay draft and try to recall and record the sensory details you associate with this moment.

Moment in my story: _____

Sense	Sensory Details
Sight	
Smell	
Sound	
Taste	
Touch	

Reread your reflective essay draft and apply the same critical eye for examples of showing and telling in your own sentences as you did with the sample essay "Reflecting on a Box." Underline where you have done a good job showing readers what occurred. Put squiggly lines under phrases and sentences that will need to be revised. Use the chart on this page to help you add sensory details.

As you read circle any abstract verbs in your draft that need to be replaced with more specific and concrete verbs.

 **KNOW IT** Make your descriptions more vivid by using specific verbs and descriptions that appeal to your readers' senses. Include details that invite readers to see, hear, taste, touch, and feel what you and others did when the events you describe occurred.

LESSON 5 Revising

The word *revise* comes from the Latin verb *revisere* meaning "to look at again" or "to visit again." That is what you will be doing in this lesson—looking at your draft with a critical eye, visiting it again in order to make improvements.

Three of the most basic moves to make when revising a draft are adding, subtracting, and moving things around.

- **Add** to your essay if you find places that seem undeveloped, ideas that are unexplained, or descriptions that appear bare.

- **Subtract or delete** if you find a passage that goes on for too long or a sentence that is wordy. Wordy sentences often include unnecessary phrases that add nothing to the meaning of the sentence. Clear, **concise** writing can express a great deal in a few words. A brief expression of ideas is almost always preferable to a long-winded explanation.

  It's easy to find yourself writing wordy phrases when drafting because your mind is focused on the content of what you are trying to say. During the revision process try to delete all such empty phrasings. Here are a few expressions to be on the lookout for.

Wordy phrases	Concise revisions
the reason why is that owing to the fact that because of the fact that in view of the fact that	because
Miguel is a man who likes	Miguel likes
in my own personal opinion	I believe
in a timely manner	promptly
reached a decision	decided
at the present time at this point in time	now
during the course of the night	during the night
made reference to	referred to
during the time that	while
an adequate number of	enough
despite the fact that	despite
in close proximity to	near

You also want to avoid **redundancy**. Redundant expressions say the same thing twice. Think for a moment about the phrase "totally unique." An object is either one-of-a-kind or it isn't. The adverb "totally" adds nothing to the meaning of "unique" and is therefore redundant.

Redundant Expression	Revision
totally unique	unique
refer back to	refer to
exactly identical	identical
individual persons	individuals
true facts	facts
period of time	period

- **Move things around** if you find that certain details would be more effective either earlier or later in the essay. Did you include too much reflection in your introduction and need to move these sentences to your conclusion? Would a different moment from your autobiographical incident work better for an eye-catching opening sentence? Working on a computer can make such changes a snap, allowing you to cut and paste whole sections of your draft to see how the move affects the essay as a whole.

EXAMPLE

Here is a sample student draft that is wordy in places, needs elaboration in others, and includes sentences that would work better if moved to another spot in the essay. See if you can identify where the draft needs revision and mark your revisions on the page. Then compare your ideas with the corrected version that follows.

Sample student reflective essay

Use the Common Editing Marks on p. 231 to mark your revisions to this essay.

I am always a little bit sad when it snows. Why you ask? Because my godfather died shoveling snow. One morning after a heavy Chicago snowfall Joe went out with a big shovel to clear his driveway. Joe Crosetto, my beloved godfather, was only 50 years old. It was still dark out with lots of heavy clouds in the sky, and about 2 feet of heavy, wet snow had accumulated in the driveway and on the sidewalks. It would be the last day of Joe's life. He hadn't even had his cup of coffee yet.

Joe started out that morning with a big smile. He had had a family party at his house the night before. His specialty was pizza that he made himself with about a pound of Italian sausage on every pizza. He made the dough and the sauce himself and always had about ten or so pizzas in his freezer so that nobody would ever go hungry at his house. We all had a wonderful time together eating Joe's pizzas. Everyone was talking and laughing and sharing stories about what we had been doing. When we left the weather was turning nasty, but we all got home safely.

The next morning the call came from Joe's wife. Joe had gone out to clear the driveway before going in to work. When he didn't come in after an hour, she went out to look for him. There he was on the ground. She called the paramedics, but it was too late. I can't see snow now without thinking about that tragic morning.

Revised reflective essay

I am always a little bit sad when it snows. Why you ask? Snow probably reminds you of Christmas and sled rides, days off from school and happy snowball fights, but my godfather died shoveling snow. One morning after a heavy Chicago snowfall Joe went out with a big shovel to clear his driveway. ~~Joe Crosetto, my beloved godfather, was only 50 years old.~~ It was still dark out with lots of heavy clouds in the sky, and about 2 feet of heavy, wet snow had accumulated in the driveway and on the sidewalks. It would be the last day of Joe's life. ~~He hadn't even had his cup of coffee yet.~~

Joe started out that morning with a big smile. He shouted to his wife, who was also named Jo, that he'd be back in for a cup of coffee in about 15 minutes. He had had a family party at his house the night before. ~~His specialty~~

Elaborating the associations that most people have with snow would help readers contrast these typical feelings about snow with the writer's memories.

This sentence about the godfather's age feels out of place here. Move to the end of the essay in order to emphasize the sadness of his passing at such a relatively young age.

This reference to the cup of coffee would be better placed in the second paragraph where the writer is telling the story about the day Joe died.

The moved sentence could be elaborated to add more concrete detail about Joe's morning.

This section on the pizzas is wordy and needs revision in order to keep the focus of the essay on the writer's godfather.

~~was pizza that he made himself with about a pound of Italian sausage on every pizza. He made the dough and the sauce himself and always had about ten or so pizzas in his freezer so that nobody would ever go hungry at his house.~~ Homemade pizza was Joe's specialty, and his freezer always held a dozen extras—just in case. We all had a wonderful time together eating Joe's pizzas. Everyone was talking and laughing and sharing stories about what we had been doing. When we left the weather was turning nasty, but we all got home safely.

Wordy

Needs further elaboration to paint the scene.

The next morning the call came from Joe's wife. Joe had gone out to clear the driveway before ~~going in to~~ work. When he didn't come in after an hour, she went out to look for him. There he was on the ground. Joe was face down in the snow with his shovel in hand. The driveway was clear. She called the paramedics, but it was too late. Joe Crosetto, my beloved godfather, was only 50 years old. I can't see snow now without thinking about that tragic morning.

Try It

On the lines below, add detail and elaboration to the underdeveloped sample sentences.

1. The house felt empty.

_____

_____

_____

2. Jacelyn was angry.

_____

_____

_____

3. I needed help.

_____

_____

_____

Revise the following sentences to eliminate wordiness and redundancies.

1. Due to the fact that many people are afraid of flying, airlines make reference to crashes at sea as "water landings."

   _____

   _____

   _____

2. In my own personal opinion, it is always better to find a totally unique present to give on the occasion of a birthday than a gift certificate.

   _____

   _____

   _____

3. If you refer back to your notes, you will see an adequate number of true facts laid out for you on the French Revolution.

   _____

   _____

   _____

Revise the following paragraph, marking with arrows where sentences need to be moved so that the essay reads more clearly and coherently. Write your corrected paragraph on the lines that follow.

As a twin, I have lived through life's milestones at the same time and in the same context as did my brother. For example, when my brother fractured his wrist at the beginning of the tennis season, it was as if I had fractured my own wrist. I had played tennis with him for ten years, and I knew what not being able to play meant to him. I felt his disappointment, and this "identical twin empathy" has helped me grow as a person. Together we transitioned from middle school to high school, tried out for the tennis team, learned to drive, and began to date. Being a twin has given me the unique perspective of experiencing life through the eyes of another person. Because we experienced these events together, I was very in tune with how he was affected by them.

_____

_____

_____

_____

_____

_____

_____

_____

_____

_____

_____

_____

_____

_____

_____

_____

_____

_____

The following guidelines will help focus your revision of your draft.

> **[TIP]**
>
> Try to be as objective as you can about your writing. Read your draft as if it were written by your best friend, whom you really want to help do well.

1. Use a colored pen to mark places where your draft needs further development with a large **ADD**. If the draft isn't at least two pages long, it most certainly will need more work. Longer isn't always better, but development of ideas is an essential feature of competent writing.

2. Cross out passages that distract from your main point. It may be hard to delete sentences you worked hard to craft, but if they don't serve your reflective purpose, your essay will be stronger without them.

3. Circle any wordy or redundant phrases and revise them for conciseness.

4. Use arrows to indicate sections of your draft that you want to move from one place to another.

5. Check the balance of your storytelling and reflective commentary by highlighting all the reflection with a yellow marker. If more than 75% of your essay is devoted to an autobiographical incident, the balance is off. Reflective commentary should make up between 25% and 50% of your draft. Revise the draft to establish a better balance.

Ask for Help

Imagine that you have a friend or family member willing to read your draft and offer suggestions. Use the following **template** to write a note asking for help. Explaining to someone else where you think your draft needs work can help you figure out what changes to make as you revise. (If you want, you can write a letter back to yourself from your friend or family member with suggestions on how to address your problem areas!)

Dear _____ (your friend or family member's name)

    In this essay I am trying to _____

_____

_____

_____

    At the moment I am still struggling to _____

_____

_____

    I am also worried about _____

_____

_____

_____

    Do you have any advice for me about how to _____

_____

_____ ?

Thanks for your help.

Sincerely,

_____

(your name)

Reflective Essay Rubric

Use the rubric on the following page to help guide your reflective writing. As you read your draft, consider changes that would help your finished essay match the description in category 5.

REFLECTIVE ESSAY RUBRIC (5-point scale)

A 5 reflective essay explores the significance of personal experiences, events, or concerns and analyzes the connections between specific incidents and broader ideas, illustrating the writer's beliefs or generalizations about life. The writer describes personal experiences in vivid sensory detail, recounting events clearly and concisely, and maintains a balance between the description of incidents and insightful reflective commentary. The essay is focused, demonstrates a clear sense of purpose and audience, and uses appropriate tone and style. Organization is coherent with appropriate transitions between and within paragraphs to create a cohesive whole. Word choice is precise, sentences are varied, and grammatical errors are rare or absent.

A 4 reflective essay presents a competent description of personal experiences, events or concerns and an analysis of their significance. The writer describes personal experiences coherently and with appropriate detail. The essay generally maintains its focus and demonstrates a sense of purpose, tone, and audience. Organization is generally clear with transitions between paragraphs. A competency with language is apparent. Word choice is appropriate and sentences are sometimes varied. Some errors in sentence structure, usage, and mechanics are present.

A 3 reflective essay presents a minimally competent description of personal experiences, events, or concerns. The writer offers some commentary on their significance, but the essay lacks analysis and may consist largely of storytelling. The essay generally maintains its focus with minor digressions. Its sense of purpose, tone, and audience may be unclear. Organization is clear enough to follow. A limited control of language is apparent. Word choice is imprecise and sentences may be poorly constructed or confusing. Errors in sentence structure, usage, and mechanics are present.

A 2 reflective essay presents a weakly developed description of personal experiences, events, or concerns. The writer offers minimal and/or inappropriate commentary to connect personal experiences with larger ideas. The essay demonstrates significant problems in one or more of the following areas that make the writer's ideas difficult to follow: unclear focus, lack of organization, weak controlling idea, and redundancy. Style and tone may be inappropriate for the audience. Writing demonstrates weak control of language. A pattern of errors in grammar and mechanics significantly interferes with meaning.

A 1 reflective essay presents an ineffective description of personal experiences, events, or concerns. Ideas and commentary are absent, irrelevant, unsupported by evidence, or incomprehensible. The essay demonstrates significant problems that make the writer's ideas difficult to follow and lacks focus and organization. Style and tone are inappropriate for the audience. Writing demonstrates poor control of language. Errors in grammar and mechanics are pervasive and obstruct meaning.

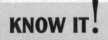

KNOW IT! Good writing requires careful revision. Once you have a draft down on paper, it's time to think about what needs to be added, what needs to be deleted, and what needs to be moved around.

LESSON 6 Editing

[TIP]

Keep a list of the mistakes that you typically make and check carefully for these personal pitfalls as you edit.

Just as you check yourself in the mirror before leaving home—Is my hair sticking up in the back? Does this jacket look better buttoned or unbuttoned?—you want to check your writing before sending it out into the world. Mistakes in your writing matter. You will be judged for correctness just as much as for your content. The following editing exercises will teach you how to proofread your work efficiently.

When proofreading your essay, you search for errors and correct them. Most writers have particular mistakes that they know they make often and learn to be constantly on the lookout for. Some of your mistakes may be simple careless errors like omitting or repeating a word. Other mistakes may be both more difficult to spot and more serious errors. Mistakes with pronouns fall into this second category.

A **pronoun** is a part of speech that replaces nouns or other pronouns. Personal pronouns refer to specific people or things and change their form in order to agree with the nouns they replace, which are referred to as **antecedents**. When editing you want to make sure that every pronoun agrees in number and gender with its antecedent. It is also critical to use the correct person and case.

For more information on **pronouns**, including a complete pronoun chart, see p. 220.

Number: singular or plural (*I* or *we*, *he* or *they*)

Gender: masculine, feminine, or neuter (*he*, *she*, or *it*)

Person: first person (*I*, *we*), second person (*you*), third person (*he*, *she*, *they*)

Case: There are three cases in English:

1. **Subjective:** used for the subject of a sentence or clause
   Examples: <u>She</u> fell in the pond.

   <u>Who</u> is at the door?

2. **Objective:** used as the direct object of the verb or the object of the preposition
   Examples: Joseph pulled <u>her</u> out of the pond. (direct object)

   Marquis didn't see the pond in front of <u>him</u>. (object of the preposition)

   For <u>whom</u> did you buy that sandwich? (object of the preposition)

3. **Possessive:** used to show possession as either a direct object or as an adjective modifying a noun
   Examples: That book is <u>mine</u>. (object possessive)

   <u>My</u> clothes got wet. (adjective possessive)

Reflexive pronouns are used when the object of a sentence is the same as the subject, as in "She hurt <u>herself</u>;" when the object of a preposition refers to the subject, as in "She was talking to <u>herself</u> when it happened;" and for emphasis, as in "She did it <u>herself</u>."

Though people often make mistakes with the following pronouns in casual conversation, every one of these pronouns takes a singular verb:

For more information on **subject/verb agreement**, see p. 222.

- *each*
  Many individuals are in trouble, but **each** <u>is</u> going to have to solve the problem alone.

- *either*
  Either of those shirts <u>is</u> appropriate to wear tonight.

- *everyone*
  Everyone <u>is</u> coming to the party in costume.

- *everybody*
  Everybody <u>needs</u> to bring a friend along.

- *neither*
  Neither of them <u>wants</u> to drive.

- *nobody*
  Nobody <u>is</u> dressing up as a clown this year.

- *someone*
  Someone <u>is</u> sure to bring chips and dip.

<u>EXAMPLE</u>

Choose the correct pronoun in each of the sentences below. Then check your answers.

1. A player on that championship-winning team should have no worries about (his/their) future in sports.

2. Neither Timo nor (I/me) agreed with the judges about who was the best dancer.

3. When I left, I handed all the extra food to Dominic and (him/he).

4. Tony was so worried about (who/whom) he should help first that he ended up not helping anyone.

5. The five ladies argued violently over (who/whom) should go first.

6. No one in the car seemed to know (their/his or her) way around the neighborhood.

[TIP]

When a pronoun is used along with another noun or name, ignore the first noun and see what would sound right if the pronoun stood alone.

7. Everybody I know had problems with (their/his or her) car this morning after the ice storm.

8. Come along for the ride with Akilah and (I/me).

9. With Doreen, Marcus, and (she/her) in tow, Grandpa Charles headed towards supermarket.

10. The decision was something only you and (I/me) could make.

11. If you bump into my neighbors in the grocery store, please ask (him/them) to pick up a loaf of bread for me.

12. Despite (her/its) age, my 80-year-old mother is still quite active.

13. Speak for (yourself/herself) when you say you don't want any lunch!

14. These forms are complicated, but I think I can fill them in by (themselves/myself).

Answers:

1. **his** (singular—agrees with "a player")

2. **I** (subjective case—ignore "Neither Troy nor")

3. **him** (objective case—pronoun shows who is receiving the verb action)

4. **whom** (objective case—object of the preposition "about")

5. **who** (subjective case—pronoun is the one going first)

6. **his or her** (singular—agrees with "No one")

7. **his or her** (singular—agrees with "Everybody")

8. **me** (objective case—object of the preposition "with")

9. **her** (objective case—ignore "Doreen" and "Toby," object of the preposition "with")

10. **I** (subjective case—ignore "you," pronoun is making the decision)

11. **them** (plural—agrees with "neighbors")

12. **her** (feminine—"mother" is a female)

13. **yourself** (second person—agrees with "you")

14. **myself** (first person singular—agrees with "I")

Proofreading Practice

The following paragraph contains mechanical errors of many different types: spelling, punctuation, subject-verb agreement, and pronoun usage. Practice your proofreading skills by finding and correcting the mistakes.

[TIP]

As you proofread this paragraph, move a pencil under each line as you read. This will help focus your eyes on every word.

Sold, the 2006 National Book Award winner in the young adult catigory by Patricia McCormick, records a year in the life of the fictional Lamisha, a 13-year-old girl sold into prostitution. The author traveled to Nepal and India; to hear the heart-breaking stories of young women who suffered this ordeal and survived. Told as a series of short poems and stories, the book will take you breath away. Should we protect young readers from such horrors. Or should young readers learn about social evils in the hope that she might help prevent such horrors from continuing? Censors would have public schools and libraries cleanse its shelves of all but uplifting stories. According to the American Library Association, last year their were 760 challenges to individual books. What occurs is that a parent will object to the subject matter or language in a book and demand that the school board remove them from school library. Parents have authority over their own child's reading material and should excercise this right when they feel a book is objectionible, but he does not have the right to dictate what other children may choose to read.

Corrected Paragraph

Sold, the 2006 National Book Award winner in the young adult category by Patricia McCormick, records a year in the life of the fictional Lamisha, a 13-year-old girl sold into prostitution. The author traveled to Nepal and India to hear the heart-breaking stories of young women who suffered this ordeal and survived. Told as a series of short poems and stories, the book will take your breath away. Should we protect young readers from such horrors? Or should young readers learn about social evils in the hope that they might help prevent such horrors from continuing? Censors would have public schools and libraries cleanse their shelves of all but uplifting stories. According to the American Library Association, last year there were 760 challenges to individual books. What occurs is that a parent will object to the subject matter or language in a book and demand that the school board remove the book from the school library. Parents have authority over their own child's reading material and should exercise this right when they feel a book is objectionable, but they do not have the right to dictate what other children may choose to read.

Try It

Read your draft slowly, checking for any and all errors in spelling, punctuation, subject-verb agreement, fragments, run-ons, and pronoun usage. Correct the mistakes.

To check for agreement between pronouns and their antecedents (the nouns they stand for), circle each pronoun in your draft. Then ask yourself:

- What is the noun that the pronoun replaces?

- Is that noun singular or plural?

- Is that noun masculine, feminine, or neutral?

- Is the pronoun used as a subject or an object in the sentence?

[TIP]

Don't rely on a spell-check program to find all your spelling errors. Sometimes the words the program suggests as replacements aren't the words you actually want.

KNOW IT! Problems with pronouns are common errors in writing, but they can be difficult to spot. Make sure that each of your pronouns matches its antecedent in number, gender, person, and case. Editing your writing will help ensure that your essay receives the attention and the grade it deserves. Proofread slowly and carefully to find all the errors.

Wrap It Up

Use the rubric below (introduced in lesson 3.5) to self-evaluate your essay before handing it in.

REFLECTIVE ESSAY RUBRIC (5-point scale)

A 5 reflective essay explores the significance of personal experiences, events, or concerns and analyzes the connections between specific incidents and broader ideas, illustrating the writer's beliefs or generalizations about life. The writer describes personal experiences in vivid sensory detail, recounting events clearly and concisely, and maintains a balance between the description of incidents and insightful reflective commentary. The essay is focused, demonstrates a clear sense of purpose and audience, and uses appropriate tone and style. Organization is coherent with appropriate transitions between and within paragraphs to create a cohesive whole. Word choice is precise, sentences are varied, and grammatical errors are rare or absent.

A 4 reflective essay presents a competent description of personal experiences, events or concerns and an analysis of their significance. The writer describes personal experiences coherently and with appropriate detail. The essay generally maintains its focus and demonstrates a sense of purpose, tone, and audience. Organization is generally clear with transitions between paragraphs. A competency with language is apparent. Word choice is appropriate and sentences are sometimes varied. Some errors in sentence structure, usage, and mechanics are present.

A 3 reflective essay presents a minimally competent description of personal experiences, events, or concerns. The writer offers some commentary on their significance, but the essay lacks analysis and may consist largely of storytelling. The essay generally maintains its focus with minor digressions. Its sense of purpose, tone, and audience may be unclear. Organization is clear enough to follow. A limited control of language is apparent. Word choice is imprecise and sentences may be poorly constructed or confusing. Errors in sentence structure, usage, and mechanics are present.

A 2 reflective essay presents a weakly developed description of personal experiences, events, or concerns. The writer offers minimal and/or inappropriate commentary to connect personal experiences with larger ideas. The essay demonstrates significant problems in one or more of the following areas that make the writer's ideas difficult to follow: unclear focus, lack of organization, weak controlling idea, and redundancy. Style and tone may be inappropriate for the audience. Writing demonstrates weak control of language. A pattern of errors in grammar and mechanics significantly interferes with meaning.

A 1 reflective essay presents an ineffective description of personal experiences, events, or concerns. Ideas and commentary are absent, irrelevant, unsupported by evidence, or incomprehensible. The essay demonstrates significant problems that make the writer's ideas difficult to follow and lacks focus and organization. Style and tone are inappropriate for the audience. Writing demonstrates poor control of language. Errors in grammar and mechanics are pervasive and obstruct meaning.

My paper should score a: _____

Use the following questions to help you reflect upon what you have learned in this unit.

1. What was the most challenging thing about writing a reflective essay? Why?

_____

_____

_____

_____

_____

2. Which part of the assignment did you enjoy the most? Why?

_____

_____

_____

_____

_____

3. How do you plan to use what you learned about showing versus telling in your future writing?

_____

_____

_____

_____

_____

4. Which aspects of pronoun usage do you know you need to be on the lookout for when editing future essays?

_____

_____

_____

_____

5. Do you enjoy writing reflective essays? Why or why not?

_____

_____

_____

_____

UNIT 4 Writing on Demand

You might not think of it this way, but almost every time you put pen to paper you are **writing on demand**. Whether responding to an e-mail, writing on a social networking site, or jotting a note to a friend, most everyday writing involves writing quickly. Poets may have hours to contemplate each word and phrase, but the rest of us write with the clock ticking.

Much of your college writing will require you to write under a time limit. This most often occurs in the pressure-filled essay-exam setting. You may have only a short window to write an essay that adequately demonstrates your mastery of the material.

When writing under the pressure of time, you don't have the luxury of getting halfway through only to realize you want to take a different approach. Therefore, you want to be certain that you fully understand what the **prompt** is asking BEFORE you create your thesis and start to write. Given that the clock is ticking, writers often rush through reading the question and begin writing before they have figured out what it is they are being asked to do. Calmness and proper planning up front will save you time in the end. Discipline yourself to read the prompt at least three times before you begin writing.

1. **Skim to get the main thrust of the prompt.** What is the subject you have been asked to write about? What are you being asked to do? Do you need to take a stand on an issue? Who is the audience? If no audience is identified in the prompt, what can you assume about who will be reading your essay?

2. **Reread, checking for multiple steps in the question.** Are you being asked to do more than one thing in this essay, for example to interpret and evaluate or to summarize and critique? If you write to only one aspect of the question, you may only receive partial credit for your essay.

3. **Read the prompt a third time, circling the verbs and underlining other important words.** Action verbs are your clearest indicators of what you are expected to do in the essay. Be sure you understand the distinctions among the following verbs commonly used in writing prompts.

   ANALYZE: Break the subject down into parts and explain the various parts. Explain the why and how of a subject.

   ARGUE: Offer reasons that will persuade a reader to do or believe as you do; appeal to a reader's reason and feelings. PERSUADE is sometimes used in place of *argue*.

   COMPARE: Show how two things are similar; include details or examples.

   CONTRAST: Show how two things are different; include details or examples.

CRITIQUE: Point out both the positive and negative aspects of the subject.

DESCRIBE: Write about the subject so the reader can easily visualize it; tell how it looks or happens, including who, what, when, where, and why.

DISCUSS: Give a complete and detailed answer, including important characteristics and main points.

EVALUATE: Offer an opinion of the value of the subject, including its strengths and weaknesses.

ILLUSTRATE: Make a point and offer specific examples to support it.

INTERPRET: Explain the meaning of a reading passage; discuss the results or effects of something.

PERSUADE: Offer reasons that will convince a reader to do or believe as you do; appeal to a reader's reason and feelings. ARGUE is sometimes used in place of *persuade*.

RESPOND: State your overall reaction to the subject, then support your opinion with reasons and examples, referring back to the reading.

SUMMARIZE: Briefly cover the main points of a reading passage; exclude personal opinions.

4. **Restate the prompt.** Once you have a clear idea of what the prompt is asking you to do, the next step is to restate the prompt in your own words. Along with checking your own understanding of the question, restating will help to cement the prompt in your memory and help you from drifting away from the topic in the course of your writing.

EXAMPLE

Sample Writing Prompt

In many schools across the nation, students are being required to complete a certain number of hours of volunteer community service in order to graduate. What do you think about this? Is community service an essential part of a student's education or should volunteer work be just that—voluntary?

Write an essay in which you persuade readers of your opinion regarding requiring community service for graduation. Be sure to use specific reasons and examples to support your opinion.

1. **Skim to get the main thrust of the prompt.**

The prompt is divided into two sections. The first describes the situation you are being asked to respond to. The questions are an attempt to stimulate interest in the prompt. The second section gives you directions for writing and indicates the form your response should take (an essay). No audience is indicated, but you should assume that the conditions under which you have been asked to write to this prompt (for a state test, for placement in a course, etc.) determine that the audience will be made up of adults in a position to judge the quality of your writing.

2. **Reread, checking for multiple steps in the question.**

The prompt asks you to take a pro or con stand on the issue of required community service and to express your opinion in an essay with the intent to persuade others to think as you do. The prompt specifically asks for reasons and examples to support your thesis.

3. **Read the prompt a third time, circling the verbs and underlining other important words.**

The key action verb in this prompt is "persuade." Notice, too, that you are asked "to use specific reasons" and "to support your opinion." You need to do more than simply say what you think about community service. You are going to have to **argue** in support of your position using "reasons and examples." Given that the prompt uses plural forms here, it is wise to assume that you should provide more than one reason and more than one example.

4. **Restate the prompt in your own words.**

Imagine that you wanted to explain to a friend what you were being asked to write about. How would you paraphrase the question? Explain what it is you have been asked to do. For example, "This prompt asks me to write about how I feel about schools requiring students to do community service to graduate. I have to say whether I am for or against it and then defend my position with reasons and examples. The essay is supposed to persuade a reader to agree with me."

Try It

Use the four steps described above to unpack the following sample writing prompts. Prompts come in many different forms. Some open with a quotation that is meant to get you thinking about an issue but that does not need to be directly responded to. Others open with a passage that you must analyze before moving on to your own position or point of view. Read and reread the prompt carefully to make sure you understand what you are being asked to do.

Remember to work carefully through all four steps when unpacking the prompts.

Sample Prompt #1:

In 1968, artist Andy Warhol stated that everyone will be famous for 15 minutes. Warhol was referring to the temporary nature of fame and the public's short attention span.

In a well-developed essay, describe and defend your views about fame and celebrity. You may choose to discuss how fame affects an individual, how famous men and women affect others, or how you seek fame in your own life. Support your position with reasoning and examples taken from your reading, studies, experience, or observations.

1. What are you being asked to do? Who is your audience?

_____

_____

_____

_____

2. Is there more than one part to this prompt? If so, what is the second thing you need to address in your essay?

_____

_____

_____

_____

3. What are the key verbs and phrases in this prompt?

_____

_____

_____

_____

4. Paraphrase the prompt in your own words.

_____

_____

_____

_____

_____

_____

_____

Sample Prompt #2:

What is an important goal that you hope to achieve in the next few years?

In a well-developed essay, identify one goal and explain how you plan to achieve it. Use personal observations, experience, and knowledge to support your points.

1. What are you being asked to do? Who is your audience?

   _____

   _____

   _____

   _____

2. Is there more than one part to this prompt? If so, what is the second thing you need to address in your essay?

   _____

   _____

   _____

   _____

3. What are the key verbs and phrases in this prompt?

   _____

   _____

   _____

   _____

4. Paraphrase the prompt in your own words.

   _____

   _____

   _____

   _____

   _____

   _____

   _____

   _____

   _____

Sample Prompt #3:

Inventions change our lives in many ways. Big inventions like television, computers, or microwave ovens have had such a huge impact on our culture that they seem to overshadow the smaller inventions, like ballpoint pens, headphones, or calculators.

Write an essay in which you compare the "big" inventions to the "small" ones. Which inventions play a more important role in your daily life? Be sure to provide reasons to support your position. You may use the examples of the inventions above or come up with some of your own.

1. What are you being asked to do? Who is your audience?

_____

_____

_____

_____

2. Is there more than one part to this prompt? If so, what is the second thing you need to address in your essay?

_____

_____

_____

_____

3. What are the key verbs and phrases in this prompt?

_____

_____

_____

_____

4. Paraphrase the prompt in your own words.

_____

_____

_____

_____

_____

_____

_____

[TIP]

Many prompts ask you to take a position and then defend your point of view. Don't spend a lot of time debating in your head which side to take. Your essay will be judged based on the quality of your argument, not which side you take in the argument.

Sample Prompt #4:

Who are our heroes? The media attention given to celebrities suggests that they are today's heroes, yet ordinary people perform extraordinary acts of courage every day that go virtually unnoticed. Are these people the real heroes?

Write an essay in which you define heroism and argue who you think our heroes really are—mass-media stars, ordinary people, or maybe both. Be sure to use examples of specific celebrities, other people you have heard or read about, or people from your own community to support your position.

1. What are you being asked to do? Who is your audience?

_____

_____

_____

_____

2. Is there more than one part to this prompt? If so, what is the second thing you need to address in your essay?

_____

_____

_____

_____

3. What are the key verbs and phrases in this prompt?

_____

_____

_____

_____

4. Paraphrase the prompt in your own words.

_____

_____

_____

_____

_____

_____

_____

Sample Prompt #5:

In a well-developed essay, explain how technology both makes life easier and promotes laziness. You can discuss how technology influences your daily life, how it affects others you know, or the need for technology in modern life. Support your position with sound reasoning and examples taken from your reading, studies, experience, or observations.

1. What are you being asked to do? Who is your audience?

   _____

   ._____

   _____

   _____

2. Is there more than one part to this prompt? If so, what is the second thing you need to address in your essay?

   _____

   _____

   _____

   _____

3. What are the key verbs and phrases in this prompt?

   _____

   _____

   _____

   _____

4. Paraphrase the prompt in your own words.

   _____

   _____

   _____

   _____

   _____

 **KNOW IT!** The first step when writing on demand is to be sure that you understand exactly what the prompt is asking you to do.

Does a blank sheet of paper terrify you? Do you sometimes find yourself at a loss for ideas, unsure of what to say next? The best way to get past this kind of writer's block is to start with a plan. This lesson will demonstrate how to sketch out a structure for your essay that will help keep you on track, on topic, and on your way!

No matter how enthusiastic you are about a test question or how much you feel you have to say in response to a prompt, it is a good idea to take a few minutes to jot down the main points you plan to make in your essay. Often when working under the pressure of time, writers find that they spend more time than they mean to on one example, particularly if the example is a personal anecdote. By the time they come to the end of their story, they have forgotten what it was that they wanted to say next in support of their thesis.

A simple way to avoid this common danger is to pause and lay out a plan for your essay BEFORE you begin to write. In a 25-minute or even a 55-minute period, you won't have time to construct a detailed outline like the ones described in previous lessons, but you will have time to makes quick notes. Not only will such notes keep you from forgetting important points, they may also help you come up with ideas. Use scratch paper for these notes or simply sketch them out in the margins of your test booklet. Take care, though. Be sure to notice in the instructions for the timed test where you are and aren't allowed to write. You could lose major points, or even not get credit at all, if you write in the wrong part of the booklet. If your writing test is conducted on a computer, pay attention to where—and if—the software makes room for prewriting. Some programs do, some don't. If yours doesn't, ask the teacher or test administrator if prewriting is allowed on scratch paper.

Two or three minutes spent planning your essay can make a huge difference in being able to take full advantage of the time allowed for writing. The less time you spend chewing on an eraser and staring into space, the more time you will have to write.

EXAMPLES

Writing plans can take any number of forms. Here are a few examples of **graphic organizers** that you may find useful for organizing your thoughts quickly. The key is to find and use a style that works for you and your topic. Don't waste time trying to force your thoughts into an organizer that just isn't working.

Cluster Diagram

Supporting Point #1:

Drivers on cell phones are less likely to hear the sirens of emergency vehicles.

Supporting Point #2:

Drivers on cell phones aren't focused on the road or the other cars (accidents more likely).

Thesis:

States should outlaw use of cell phones while driving.

Supporting Point #3:

Drivers on cell phones only have one hand on the wheel, which makes it difficult to maneuver quickly and safely.

<u>**Flow Chart**</u>

Main Idea:

Year-round school is better for students.

Supporting Point #1:

No long summer means less forgotten (no learning gap).

Supporting Point #2:

Less time spent reviewing forgotten material means more instructional time on new content.

Supporting Point #3 or Concession:

It may make it harder on parents' schedules at first, but they should eventually adjust.

Conclusion:

For the benefit of all students, schools should use a year-round schedule.

Venn Diagram

TOPIC: _____ Year-Round School Year vs. Standard Calendar School Year _____

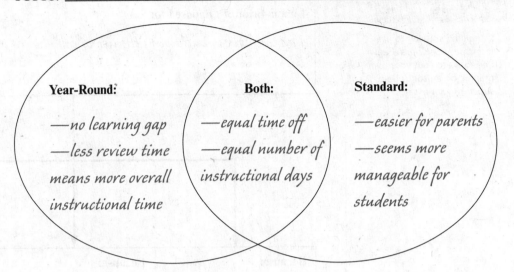

Year-Round:

—_no learning gap_
—_less review time_
means more overall
instructional time

Both:

—_equal time off_
—_equal number of_
instructional days

Standard:

—_easier for parents_
—_seems more_
manageable for
students

[TIP]

If you are comparing more than two things, simply add a third or fourth circle to the **Venn diagram**.

Problem/ Solution Chart

PROBLEM		
	Who?	_people who drive while talking on their cell phones_
	What?	_practice unsafe driving techniques and more likely to cause or be in accident_
	Why?	_their attention is on the conversation, they are not handling the vehicle safely_
SOLUTION		
	Remedy:	_outlaw talking on cell phones while driving_
	Results:	_safer driving conditions, fewer traffic accidents_
	Future effects:	_insurance companies would save money, people would become more aware of how their actions affect their environments_

Taking a Stand (Pro or Con)

[TIP]

Don't limit yourself to the forms provided here. Feel free to sketch out your own graphic organizer to help structure your essay.

I am in favor of / opposed to:

I am in favor of outlawing the use of cell phones when driving.

Because:
When people are talking on the phone, they can't hear sirens or other warning sounds.

Because:
When people talk on the phone while driving, they aren't thinking about what is happening on the road and can easily get in an accident.

Because:
When people hold a phone in their hands, they have only one hand on the steering wheel, so they can't turn quickly and carefully.

Try It

Turn back to the prompts you analyzed in Lesson 1. Choose one to respond to and then use a graphic organizer to plan your essay. If you find that the graphic organizer you choose at first isn't a good fit for your ideas, simply choose another.

Remember, the goal is not a perfectly filled-in graphic organizer but rather a useful organizational plan that can help you work efficiently under the pressure of time.

Use the space on the following page to sketch your graphic organizer.

[TIP]

To help guide your decision about which prompt to select, consider whether you have the background knowledge to write about this topic. Passionate intensity over an issue won't be enough. You need to be able to come up with good examples.

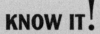

KNOW IT! When writing on demand, take a moment before beginning your essay to plan the course you want your response to take. You don't need to stick strictly to your preliminary notes when writing, but having them at hand may keep you from wasting precious minutes wondering what to write next.

Because you won't have time to revise your timed essay, it is a good idea to think about the criteria that will be used to judge your paper BEFORE you begin to write. What will scorers be looking for in your essay? What features must be present? Which errors will bring down your score?

Writing on demand is essentially the same as writing a first draft. The readers who will be evaluating your essay know you have been given only a limited amount of time to write and will take this into consideration when scoring. Though they expect a carefully organized and fully developed piece of writing, they understand that you haven't had time to revise and polish your work. While misspellings and mechanical errors do matter, the occasional mistake with a difficult word or construction is often forgiven.

Many timed writing prompts include a set of reminders or tips to help you remember the critical aspects of writing. Following the instructions for writing, you may find a list similar to the one below. You can be certain that readers will be looking for these features in your essay.

Don't forget:

- to state your position clearly.

- to anticipate and address readers' possible concerns and/or arguments against your position (for persuasive prompts).

- to present supporting points and explain how this evidence relates to your thesis.

- to separate your points into distinct paragraphs.

- to use correct grammar, spelling, punctuation, and capitalization.

In college a professor may provide you with a long list of questions based on the material covered before the day of the exam in order to help you review. On the day of the test, the professor will provide only handful of prompts from the list for you to choose from. The wise student studies all the questions and arrives for the exam prepared to write to any of them. Readers of these types of essays focus largely on content rather than style, but if your writing is disorganized or full of errors, your content will not be clear and your essay will likely lose points.

EXAMPLE
The following rubric represents the key features that readers of your essay will be looking for, as well as a description of the kind of writing that will cause your essay to receive a poor grade. Think of a score of 5 as your target.

TIMED WRITING RUBRIC (5-point scale)

A 5 timed essay responds clearly and directly to the prompt. The writer's position is explicitly stated and supported with carefully chosen and compelling evidence. Each piece of evidence is analyzed to demonstrate how it contributes to the essay's thesis. The essay is focused, demonstrates a clear sense of purpose and audience, and uses appropriate tone and style. Organization is coherent with appropriate transitions between and within paragraphs. Word choice is precise, sentences are varied, and grammatical errors are rare or absent.

A 4 timed essay adequately responds to the prompt. The writer's position is sufficiently explicit and supported with appropriate evidence. Supporting evidence is sometimes but not always analyzed to demonstrate how it contributes to the essay's thesis. The essay generally maintains its focus and demonstrates a sense of purpose, tone, and audience. Organization is generally clear with transitions between paragraphs. A competency with language is apparent. Word choice is appropriate and sentences are sometimes varied. Some errors in sentence structure, usage, and mechanics are present.

A 3 timed essay responds minimally to the prompt. The writer's position is insufficiently explicit. Supporting evidence is sketchy, undeveloped, or only partially elaborated. It is unclear how the evidence advances the writer's thesis. The essay generally maintains its focus with minor digressions. Its sense of purpose, tone, and audience may be unclear. Organization is clear enough to follow. A limited control of language is apparent. Word choice is imprecise and sentences may be poorly constructed or confusing. Errors in sentence structure, usage, and mechanics are present.

A 2 timed essay presents a weak response to the prompt. The writer takes a position but offers minimal and/or inappropriate evidence to support its thesis or responds to only one part of the prompt. The essay demonstrates significant problems in one or more of the following areas, which makes the writer's ideas difficult to follow: unclear focus, lack of organization, weak controlling idea, and redundancy. Style and tone may be inappropriate for the audience. Writing demonstrates weak control of language. A pattern of errors in grammar and mechanics significantly interferes with meaning.

A 1 timed essay presents an ineffective response to the prompt. The writer may fail to understand the prompt or fail to take a position. The essay offers little evidence to support its thesis. Ideas and explanations are absent, irrelevant, unsupported by evidence, or incomprehensible. The essay lacks focus and organization, making the writer's ideas difficult to follow. Style and tone may be inappropriate for the audience. Writing demonstrates poor control of language. Errors in grammar and mechanics are pervasive and obstruct meaning.

To make sure that you clearly understand your target, paraphrase the description for an essay that scores a 5 on this rubric. Remember that a paraphrase restates every idea and point in the original text in your own words.

_____

_____

_____

_____

_____

_____

_____

_____

_____

_____

_____

_____

_____

_____

_____

_____

_____

■ Try It

Though readers of timed writings pledge to read every word you have written, it is human nature to jump to conclusions about the quality of an essay based upon its opening sentences. Imagine you are scoring student essays and read the following opening sentences of timed essays. Do they make you want to read on? Do they suggest that the essay is likely to be strong and clear or do they seem to indicate that a weak, unfocused paper will follow? After reading each sample predict the score you think the essay is likely to earn based on the Timed Writing Rubric. Explain your score.

Student sample #1:

Literature has been alive for many years. From different cultures and languages, literature comes to us written by many different people and for many different reasons.

PREDICTED SCORE: _____

Student sample #2:

Chess, the timeless game of strategy and tactics, was founded in the arid plateaus of Ancient Persia. It mirrors the brutal competition for power between nations in a diplomatic, gentleman-like way. Although the pieces may have changed from kings to dictators, rooks to clergymen, and pawns to citizens, chess' ultimate goal has maintained the same: victory.

PREDICTED SCORE: _____

Student sample #3:

High school was awesome. I have had the greatest most memorable experiences of my life. I played a lot, partied a lot, learned, partied, and developed the things that make me who I am today.

PREDICTED SCORE: _____

Student sample #4:

Clueless is the modern day "valley girl" version of the novel *Emma*. *Emma* by Jane Austin and the 1995 movie *Clueless* tell a similar story. The main characters take on roles which allow them to go through similar life changing experiences, which can occur either in the early 1900s or the 1990s.

PREDICTED SCORE: _____

Student sample #5:

The strain from practice on the tennis court has done more than shape my muscles. It has shaped my life. I carry with me today the knowledge, skills, and habits I have learned from playing tennis at a competitive level.

PREDICTED SCORE: _____

Check your predicted scores:				
#1: 4	#2: 5	#3: 2	#4: 3	#5: 5

Reread the Timed Writing Rubric. Use the following checklist to determine which of the features described pose the greatest challenge for you when you write under pressure.

Features of Effective Timed Writing	I'm confident I can do this well.	I'm worried about doing this well.
Strong thesis statement		
Engaging opening		
Clearly organized argument		
Each paragraph has a strong topic sentence.		
Well-developed supporting paragraphs include reasons and examples.		
Supporting paragraphs include an explanation of how the evidence supports the thesis.		
Supporting paragraphs are logically ordered.		
Clear transitions between ideas within paragraphs		
Clear transitions between paragraphs		
Sentences are carefully constructed (e.g., no run-ons or fragments).		
Punctuation is accurate.		
Spelling is correct.		
Conclusion returns to the thesis and reflects on the significance of the argument.		

[TIP]

Make sure that your opening sentences are clearly expressed and free from careless errors.

[TIP]

Once you have identified your areas of weakness, review the instruction in previous lessons that deal with these features of good writing.

KNOW IT! Rubrics offer clear guidelines for effective writing. Knowing what criteria your scorers are using ahead of time will allow you to focus on the aspects of writing that are most critical for success.

The best advice for writing on demand is to relax. But how can you relax with the clock ticking and your grade—or possibly your future—in the balance? This lesson offers methods for building your confidence when writing under the pressure of time. These strategies won't totally eliminate your instinctive fears but should help you learn how to conquer them.

Many writers experience a sense of panic when faced with blank pages. Knowing that you have a limited amount of time to cover those pages with good writing only adds to the terror. The higher the stakes—for example, on a college entrance test—the greater the fear. When approaching an on-demand task, trust that you possess the skills to accomplish what is being asked of you. Remember, too, that your writing will be judged not as a revised and refined essay but as a first draft. Everyone in the room is facing the same challenge of producing an essay without the luxury of time.

The following strategies can help you produce a piece of writing that, under the circumstances, reflects your best efforts.

Strategies for Effective Timed Writing

1. Take deep breaths. Stop stressing. Don't panic.

2. Read the prompt slowly. Read it again. Circle key words. Restate the prompt in your own words to ensure that you understand what is being asked of you.

3. Don't take too long deciding how you feel about a topic. Pick one side or the other and stick with it. Do not change your mind halfway through.

4. To help you get started and to ensure that your essay stays on topic, consider borrowing language from the prompt. This will help readers of your essay notice that you are responding directly to what has been asked. Do not, however, copy whole sentences from the prompt word for word.

5. Take a few minutes to plan the structure of your essay. A shorter, clearly organized essay is much better than a long, rambling one.

6. Don't worry if others around you begin sooner or seem to be writing faster. Try not to be distracted by others in the room.

7. Don't forget to use transitional words and phrases to connect ideas between and within paragraphs.

8. Be careful not to wander from your thesis into detailed personal stories. Check yourself if you seem to be going on for too long with one supporting point.

9. Save time to write a short conclusion. Reread the prompt and what you have written so far before crafting this final paragraph.

10. Proofread your paper for missing words, misspellings, and errors that you know you make often.

[TIP]

Before you begin writing, make sure you have everything you need ready at your fingertips: scratch paper, extra pens or pencils, an eraser, tissues, and a watch.

EXAMPLE

The following essay was written under timed conditions (45 minutes) in response to the prompt you analyzed in Lesson 1.

In many schools across the nation, students are being required to complete a certain number of hours of volunteer community service in order to graduate. What do you think about this? Is community service an essential part of a student's education or should volunteer work be just that—voluntary?

Write an essay in which you persuade readers of your opinion regarding requiring community service for graduation. Be sure to use specific reasons and examples to support your opinion.

Sample Timed Essay

Across the nation many schools have instituted community service as a requirement for high school graduation. While this may seem to be a good way to help students learn about how important it is to be a contributing member of their community, I believe the new requirement is a bad idea.

First, the new requirement places unnecessary stress on students whose families depend upon them to work after school and on weekends. Sometimes this work brings in additional income to the family. Other times families need help with child care for siblings or with housework. It isn't fair that it is easier for students from rich families to complete their community service requirement than it is for students who have part-time jobs or responsibilities at home. The new graduation requirement is more of a burden for some than others. This isn't fair.

[TIP]

Notice that the writer did not list his supporting points in the first paragraph. For an essay of this length, listing them here would have seemed repetitive.

Second, too often what is supposed to be meaningful community service is instead a bunch of hours spent cleaning cages in an animal shelter or filing papers at a free clinic. This work does little to teach high school kids what it really means to give back to their community. Students do it because they have to, not because they care about the humane treatment of animals or health care. If the goal of the new requirement is to teach the importance of active, engaged citizenship, students need a wide range of choices for how they might give back to their community. Students should be able to come up with their own ideas rather than picking from a school-approved list of volunteer opportunities.

Finally, the biggest thing that is wrong with requiring community service for graduation is that volunteer work should be voluntary. As soon as schools say, "Do this," most teenagers want to do the opposite. Young people should be encouraged to volunteer in their community and to experience the pleasure that can come from helping others. This kind of experience is ruined when it is required. Most students count every minute so that when they have completed their required hours, they never return. The requirement misses the point if it doesn't result in students choosing to continue volunteering past the required hours.

Instead of instituting new graduation requirements, let's bring true volunteerism back to our community. Students should be invited, not forced, to help others. This way, the individuals who choose to volunteer their time would be doing so for the right reasons rather than simply to get it over with.

[TIP]

Timed essays do not require titles. Most scoring guides for writing on demand indicate that students will not be given extra credit for good titles nor penalized for the absence of one. Unless a title immediately comes to mind, don't waste time trying to think up one.

Identify the following common features of effective persuasive writing in the sample student essay:

- Underline language borrowed from the prompt in the introduction.
- Draw a squiggly line under the thesis statement.
- Draw a star next to any counter-arguments.
- Draw a box around supporting evidence.
- Circle transitions.
- Underline the call to action in the conclusion.

Did you find …

- **Language borrowed from the prompt:** "Across the nation many schools have instituted community service as a requirement for high school graduation." Notice that the writer did not simply copy a sentence from the prompt but rather rephrased the idea in his own words. This can be an effective way to let readers know that your essay is responding directly to the prompt.

- **Thesis statement:** "I believe the new requirement is a bad idea." While ordinarily you want to avoid expressions like "I think" or "I believe" in your writing, in this case the phrase adds emphasis to the writer's assertion of his thesis.

- **Counter-arguments:** "While this may seem to be a good way to help students learn about how important it is to be a contributing member of their community. . . ." The writer makes clear that he recognizes the reasons others may feel the new graduation requirement is a good idea. Including this concession at the beginning of the essay helps demonstrate that the writer has thought through his position carefully.

- **Supporting evidence:** Paragraphs 2, 3, and 4 include supporting evidence primarily drawn from the writer's own experience. When writing on demand you will often find that you depend on personal experience to support your claims. It is what comes to mind first. If the writer had more time to work on this draft, each of these supporting paragraphs could have been developed more fully. Given the constraint of time, the writer did the best he could to identify three distinct reasons why he believes requiring community service is not a good idea.

- **Transitions:** The writer opens each of his supporting paragraphs with a transition word—"First," "Second," and "Finally." While this may not be the most sophisticated way to unify the ideas in this essay, the writer makes clear the connections between his supporting paragraphs.

- **Concluding call to action:** "Instead of new graduation requirements, let's bring true volunteerism back to our community." The writer states clearly what it is that he believes should happen. A call to action can be an effective way to conclude a persuasive essay because it demonstrates that the writer has ideas for alternatives to the plan he criticizes.

■ Try It

Using the prompt you chose in Lesson 1 and brainstormed ideas for in Lesson 2, write an essay on the following pages. Set a timer for 45 minutes in order to see how much you can accomplish within a limited period of time.

Restate your prompt in your own words:

_____

_____

_____

_____

Use the space below to plan your essay using a graphic organizer.

Draft your timed essay.

_____

_____

_____

_____

_____

_____

_____

_____

_____

_____

_____

_____

_____

_____

_____

_____

_____

_____

_____

_____

_____

_____

_____

_____

_____

_____

KNOW IT! In order to write well under timed conditions, you need to approach the task calmly and confidently. Try to work efficiently and do not panic. You can do it. If you understand the prompt, know how you're being graded, and have a clear plan for writing, you'll be fine!

ARE YOU READY TO GO ON?

Reread your timed essay. What do you feel are its greatest strengths and weaknesses? List them below.

Strengths: _____

_____

_____

Weaknesses: _____

_____

_____

Take a moment to reflect on your experience writing on demand. On the lines below comment on how it felt to write an essay under the pressure of time. Next time, what would you do differently? What have you learned from this exercise? How might you have used the time more effectively?

_____

_____

_____

_____

_____

_____

_____

_____

_____

_____

_____

_____

_____

_____

_____

LESSON 5 Revising

Do you sometimes feel that your sentences don't quite match the thoughts inside your head? That they oversimplify the point you really want to make? Experimenting with complex sentence structures can help you express your ideas with greater clarity and precision. It will also make your writing more enjoyable to read.

For more information on the **different types of sentences**, see p. 218.

Complex ideas require complex structures. If all you want to say is, "I hate eggs," you can do so in three words lined up in a simple subject-verb-object structure. If you want to express the tiresome nature of being served a breakfast of eggs and toast day after day with little hope of variation in the foreseeable future, you need a different kind of sentence to convey your meaning. It isn't only a matter of impressing readers with your language skills; it is about expressing your full meaning. Notice the use of a semicolon in the previous sentence. This is one way you can use more complex sentence structures. Use a semicolon instead of a period when the two ideas are closely related and influence each other's meaning. The semicolon helps to convey this relationship better than two separate sentences would. The more familiar you are with the various ways sentences are constructed, the closer you will be able to come to making your writing match your thinking.

Though you may not know the terms, you use independent clauses and dependent clauses every time you write. An **independent clause** contains a subject and verb and expresses a complete thought. For example, "I hate eggs." It is called "independent" because it doesn't need anything else to make it complete; it can stand alone. A **dependent clause** contains a subject and verb but does not express a complete thought. For example, "When I eat eggs. . . ." Dependent clauses are not sentences and are easily identified by markers like *when, after, because, if, since, although, while,* and *until.* They are called "dependent" because they depend on something else to finish the thought.

Most sentences fall into one of four categories.

Sentence Type	Definition	Examples
Simple sentences	**Simple sentences** are made up of a single independent clause. They may include a compound subject or compound verb.	1. I hate eggs. 2. Mark and I make and eat waffles. (compound subject and compound verb)
Compound sentences	**Compound sentences** are made up of two or more independent clauses joined with a comma and conjunction or with a semicolon.	1. I hate eggs, and Mark hates bacon. 2. Breakfast was awful; I hate eggs.

Sentence Types	Definitions	Examples
Complex sentences	**Complex sentences** include one independent clause and one or more dependent clauses.	1. Although I look forward to the morning meal, I hate eggs. 2. Because I hate eggs and since I love cold cereal, my breakfast is simple to prepare.
Compound-complex sentences	**Compound-complex sentences** include two or more independent clauses and at least one dependent clause.	I have always hated eggs, but I still enjoy breakfast since there is always cereal in the cupboard.

EXAMPLE

To help you get into the habit of writing compound, complex, and compound-complex sentences, complete the following charts, developing the simple sentences into longer, more sophisticated sentences. The first chart has been completed for you.

Simple sentence #1 a single independent clause	*Maria loves chocolate.*
Compound sentence two or more independent clauses joined with a comma and conjunction or with a semicolon	*Maria loves chocolate, but I don't.*
Complex sentence one independent clause and one or more dependent clauses	*Because Maria loves chocolate, I made her a chocolate fudge birthday cake.*
Compound-complex sentence two or more independent clauses and at least one dependent clause	*Maria loves chocolate, but she has given it up since she got pregnant.*

Simple sentence #2 a single independent clause	*My dog ran away.*
Compound sentence two or more independent clauses joined with a comma and conjunction or with a semicolon	
Complex sentence one independent clause and one or more dependent clauses.	
Compound-complex sentence two or more independent clauses and at least one dependent clause	

Simple sentence #3 a single independent clause	*I love watching movies.*
Compound sentence two or more independent clauses joined with a comma and conjunction or with a semicolon	
Complex sentence one independent clause and one or more dependent clauses.	
Compound-complex sentence two or more independent clauses and at least one dependent clause	

[TIP]

Don't forget to include a comma before the conjunction in a compound sentence. If you use a conjunction and forget the comma, you've written a run-on sentence.

[TIP]

In complex sentences, use a comma to separate the dependent clause from the independent clause only if the dependent clause comes at the beginning of the sentence.

Passive and Active Voice

In sentences written in the active voice, the subject performs the action described by the verb. For example, "The dog bit me." The subject, the dog, is doing the biting. In sentences written in the passive voice, the subject is acted upon. For example, "I was bitten by the dog." The subject, I, is acted upon (bitten) by the dog. Sentences written in the passive voice lack the power and directness of those written in the active voice. They employ a double verb, a form of the verb "to be" and the past participle of another verb.

> ACTIVE VOICE: The policeman stopped traffic.
> PASSIVE VOICE: Traffic was stopped by the policeman.

Of course sometimes writers employ the passive voice to avoid directness.

> ACTIVE VOICE: I made a mistake.
> PASSIVE VOICE: Mistakes were made.

Rewrite the following sentences, changing them from passive voice to active voice.

1. A good time was had by everyone.

   Active Voice: _____

   _____

2. The worm was eaten by the bird.

   Active Voice: _____

   _____

3. My motorcycle is in the shop being repaired by a mechanic.

   Active Voice: _____

   _____

4. The streets surrounding the fire were blockaded by authorities in charge.

   Active Voice: _____

   _____

5. Pineapple is grown in many parts of Hawaii by plantation owners.

   Active Voice: _____

   _____

Always try to write in the active voice. It will help to make your sentences will be shorter, clearer, and less awkward.

Varied Sentence Openings

Try to vary the way you begin sentences. When too many sentences in a row begin with *The*, *There is*, *They*, *He*, or *I*, readers get bored. See for yourself what a paragraph composed of a string of simple sentences all beginning with the subject sounds like:

> The party was over. The guests began to leave. The host, Joey, was dead tired. He started picking up the empty glasses. He dropped one and it broke. He was too exhausted to clean up the mess. He left everything and headed up to bed. He took a couple of aspirin. He fell asleep immediately.

This is an extreme example, but you want to check your writing to see if too many of your sentences begin in the same manner. Changing how you begin a sentence may change the emphasis of the sentence. Think about how the following combinations of the first two sentences from the paragraph above alter their meaning.

- You could tell the party was over because the guests began to leave.
- At last the party ended and guests began to leave.
- As soon as the first guests began to leave, I knew the party was over.
- I saw a few guests begin to leave and figured the party was over.
- Fortunately, guests began to leave and the party was over.
- With great reluctance, guests began to leave; the party was over.

On the lines below see how many different ways you can combine these two simple sentences, altering the openings. Feel free to add additional words or additional detail to enliven the new sentences.

It was raining. There was a car accident.

_____

_____

_____

_____

_____

_____

_____

_____

_____

_____

_____

_____

_____

_____

_____

_____

_____

_____

_____

_____

_____

Try It

Adding variety to your sentences will make your writing livelier and more interesting to read. Turn back to your draft and use the following codes to identify the types of sentences you used. In the boxes below keep a tally of how many of each type of sentence you used.

[TIP]

Try to vary the rhythm of your writing by alternating long, complex sentences with short, simple ones.

Sentence Type	Code	Tally
Simple sentence	S	
Compound sentence	CM	
Complex sentence	CX	
Compound-complex sentence	CMX	

Passive voice	PV	
Repetitive sentence openings	RSO	

When you are done analyzing your sentences, go back and revise where necessary.

- Vary your sentence types to include all four types of sentences.
- Change passive voice to active voice whenever possible.
- Vary your sentence openings to avoid being overly repetitive. Changing your sentence type can help.

KNOW IT!

Varying the structure of your sentences will help your writing sound more sophisticated. It will also help you to express your ideas with clarity and precision. Using active voice and varied sentence beginnings will infuse your writing with energy and keep your readers interested.

LESSON 6 Editing

When first learning to drive, many people forget to use their side mirrors or turn signals when turning. These common driving errors are easily corrected with a bit of coaching and practice. The same is true in writing. By focusing on common errors, including commonly confused words, you can avoid making mistakes—even in your first draft.

Often what appears as a misspelled word in your writing is actually the correct spelling of the wrong word. These commonly confused words make up a large percentage of the errors that appear in on-demand writing. Words that sound alike but have different meanings often cause confusion for writers. Below are ten of the most commonly confused words with definitions and examples.

ACCEPT – verb meaning *to receive* I **accept** your gift with pleasure.	**EXCEPT** – preposition meaning *to take or leave out* Everyone is going to the movies **except** for Marco.
AFFECT – verb meaning *to influence* Sleepiness can severely **affect** your driving ability.	**EFFECT** – noun meaning *result* The **effects** of the bad economy are felt in every city in the country.
ITS – pronoun meaning *of* or *belonging to it* Maine is famous for **its** clam chowder.	**IT'S** – contraction for *it is* With a fresh paint job, **it's** possible for your car to look brand new.
LOSE – verb meaning (1) *to misplace*; or (2) *to not win* (1) I often **lose** my car keys. (2) I am probably going to **lose** this argument.	**LOOSE** – noun meaning *to not be tight* Since I've lost a little weight, my ring is very **loose** on my finger.
PASSED – verb, past tense of *to pass*, meaning *to have gone by* We just **passed** the street that we needed to turn right on.	**PAST** – (1) adjective meaning *belonging to a former time or place*; or (2) noun meaning a *time gone by* (1) In the **past**, I collected baseball cards, but now I collect beer mugs. (2) My library book was **past** due.
THAN – used for making comparisons Mark would rather play video games **than** watch television.	**THEN** – meaning *at that time* or *next* I ran for five miles and **then** stopped to catch my breath.

THEIR – possessive pronoun meaning *belonging to them*
Their kids usually have soccer games on Friday nights.

THERE – indicates location
Let's put our picnic blanket down over **there**.

THEY'RE – contraction meaning *they are*
Before they start work, **they're** going shopping for new clothes.

TO – preposition meaning *toward*
Mia went **to** school at night for three years.

TOO – adverb meaning (1) *also*; or (2) *excessively*
(1) Anna saw a new movie last weekend; Martine did, **too.**
(2) It was **too** cold outside to go swimming.

TWO – a number
I already have **two** dogs, and I still want another one!

WEAR – verb meaning *to be dressed in*
Because I don't look good in green, I never know what to **wear** on St. Patrick's Day.

WHERE – (1) noun or (2) adverb meaning *place* or *location*
(1) **Where** do you want to go for dinner?
(2) That is **where** the fatal accident happened last year.

YOUR – possessive adjective meaning *belonging to you*
Your paycheck is going to have a little extra bonus added to it this month.

YOU'RE – contraction meaning *you are*
You're not going to make it to work on time if you keep hitting the snooze button.

EXAMPLE

Here is a set of sentences that include commonly confused words. Select what you think is the correct word and then check your answers. Refer to the Grammar Handbook on pp. 223 if you have questions. You may want to use a dictionary as well.

1. I refused to (accept/except) her apology.

2. (Its/It's) going to be a lovely day today.

3. The community had (alot/a lot) of complaints about the old playground equipment in the park.

4. (Their/There) house was badly in need of a new paint job.

5. If you are looking for a new notebook and pen, try the (stationery/stationary) store on the corner.

6. When writing the months of the year, always begin their names with (capital/capitol) letters.

7. Whatever subject Matt talks about, he is sure to make (allusions/illusions) to football.

8. I'm often tempted to eat (to/too/two) much chocolate.

9. Everyone (accept/except) Anna remembered to wear a hat.

10. Last night Jason (lead/led) the group in song.

11. (A part/Apart) from Hillary, everyone found a seat easily.

12. I don't have enough (capital/capitol) to buy a new car right now.

13. We're looking for a new (cite/sight/site) for the town ballpark.

14. (Their/There) is going to be a huge celebration next Fourth of July in our town.

15. It's not (all right/alright) to throw garbage out of car windows.

16. Watching that horror movie had a powerful (affect/effect) on my dreams.

17. The school (principal/principle) explained her plan to renovate the gymnasium.

18. Exercise is likely to (affect/effect) your body weight.

19. "Come (hear/here)!" she yelled. "I need you right now!"

20. Maria decided to (wear/where) her sneakers and take along her heels in her purse.

21. It is a matter of (principal/principle) with me to vote in every election.

22. The dog was chasing (its/it's) tail.

23. ("Where/Wear) are you going with my hamburger?" Toni asked.

24. Jesse always blushes when anyone pays her (complements/compliments).

25. The deadline has (passed/past) for turning in a job application to the police department.

26. Please try not to (loose/lose) your temper before you hear the whole presentation.

27. On smoggy mornings it can be hard to (breath/breathe).

28. I was not (conscious/conscience) of anyone objecting to your driving.

29. It's harder to lose weight (than/then) to gain weight.

30. You won't be able to (precede/proceed) with your plans for the party unless you get some help.

Answers:

1. accept	2. It's	3. a lot	4. their	5. stationery
6. capital	7. allusions	8. too	9. except	10. led
11. Apart	12. capital	13. site	14. There	15. alright
16. effect	17. principal	18. affect	19. here	20. wear
21. principle	22. its	23. Where	24. compliments	25. passed
26. lose	27. breathe	28. conscious	29. than	30. proceed

Try It

Review the list of commonly confused words in this lesson and on pages 223–226. On the lines below copy the words you have the most difficulty keeping straight. Include hints that can help you remember which word is which, for example: the princi*pal* is your pal.

_____   _____

_____   _____

_____   _____

_____   _____

_____   _____

_____   _____

_____   _____

_____   _____

[TIP]

Thinking of special effects in a movie may help you remember to use the noun *effect* rather than the verb *affect*.

For additional practice with these commonly confused words, write example sentences in which you use the words correctly.

_____

_____

_____

_____

_____

_____

_____

_____

_____

_____

[TIP]

If you are unsure about whether *its* or *it's* is the correct usage, read the sentence aloud, saying "it is." If the sentence makes sense, you should use the contraction *it's*.

Reread your draft, checking that you have used these commonly confused words correctly.

KNOW IT!

Knowing which words are commonly misspelled—or misused—will help you avoid making those mistakes when you write your essay. If possible, keep a dictionary or personal list of commonly confused words on hand so that you can look up the right word for any situation.

Wrap It Up

Use the rubric below (introduced in lesson 4.3) to evaluate your essay before handing it in.

TIMED WRITING RUBRIC (5-point scale)

A 5 timed essay responds clearly and directly to the prompt. The writer's position is explicitly stated and supported with carefully chosen and compelling evidence. Each piece of evidence is analyzed to demonstrate how it contributes to the essay's thesis. The essay is focused, demonstrates a clear sense of purpose and audience, and uses appropriate tone and style. Organization is coherent with appropriate transitions between and within paragraphs. Word choice is precise, sentences are varied, and grammatical errors are rare or absent.

A 4 timed essay adequately responds to the prompt. The writer's position is sufficiently explicit and supported with appropriate evidence. Supporting evidence is sometimes but not always analyzed to demonstrate how it contributes to the essay's thesis. The essay generally maintains its focus and demonstrates a sense of purpose, tone, and audience. Organization is generally clear with transitions between paragraphs. A competency with language is apparent. Word choice is appropriate and sentences are sometimes varied. Some errors in sentence structure, usage, and mechanics are present.

A 3 timed essay responds minimally to the prompt. The writer's position is insufficiently explicit. Supporting evidence is sketchy, undeveloped, or only partially elaborated. It is unclear how the evidence advances the writer's thesis. The essay generally maintains its focus with minor digressions. Its sense of purpose, tone, and audience may be unclear. Organization is clear enough to follow. A limited control of language is apparent. Word choice is imprecise and sentences may be poorly constructed or confusing. Errors in sentence structure, usage, and mechanics are present.

A 2 timed essay presents a weak response to the prompt. The writer takes a position but offers minimal and/or inappropriate evidence to support its thesis or responds to only one part of the prompt. The essay demonstrates significant problems in one or more of the following areas, which makes the writer's ideas difficult to follow: unclear focus, lack of organization, weak controlling idea, and redundancy. Style and tone may be inappropriate for the audience. Writing demonstrates weak control of language. A pattern of errors in grammar and mechanics significantly interferes with meaning.

A 1 timed essay presents an ineffective response to the prompt. The writer may fail to understand the prompt or fail to take a position. The essay offers little evidence to support its thesis. Ideas and explanations are absent, irrelevant, unsupported by evidence, or incomprehensible. The essay lacks focus and organization, making the writer's ideas difficult to follow. Style and tone may be inappropriate for the audience. Writing demonstrates poor control of language. Errors in grammar and mechanics are pervasive and obstruct meaning.

My paper should score a: _____

Continue on next page.

Imagine that your younger brother will be taking a writing test tomorrow. He needs a good score to raise his grade in 8th grade English. Based on what you have learned in this unit, what advice would you give him? Use the lines below to write a note offering him advice on writing under the pressure of time.

_____

_____

_____

_____

_____

_____

_____

_____

_____

_____

_____

_____

_____

_____

_____

_____

_____

_____

_____

_____

Have you ever sat down to write an essay and felt that you had absolutely nothing to say? It happens often when students begin writing about literature. Often the reason for this is that you try to write before you figure out what you actually think about the poem, story, or book that you have been asked to write about. This lesson will help you discover what you think BEFORE you begin to write.

Writing about literature is an **analytical** task. You are not being asked to discuss what you feel about the poem or story or to tell whether or not you liked it. You are expected to demonstrate your understanding and **interpretation** of the author's message and your insight into the text. You will accomplish this by:

- organizing your ideas around a thesis statement.

- developing your ideas in reference to specific words, lines, characters, or images in the text.

- justifying your interpretation of the text with examples.

In order to do all of this, you will need to pause before writing and figure out what you think and know about the piece of literature you have been asked to analyze. One method for making this pause productive is to write a **question paper**. In a question paper you write question after question that you have about the text. Don't worry about having answers. Just record everything—every word, every image, every reference—that puzzles you. If you find yourself wondering about possible meanings or interpretations, record that as well. Let your mind roam freely over the piece, feeling free to speculate with phrases such as:

- "I wonder if …"

- "Could it be that …?"

- "What if …?"

- "Maybe the author was trying to say …"

- "It seems to me that …"

- "I suppose it's possible that …"

While this process does involve writing, it is different from drafting because what you are putting down on the page will never appear in your final essay. Instead, you are using the act of writing to discover what you think.

In this unit we focus on writing about poetry in order to offer many different examples without requiring you to read whole stories or books. However, know that all of the techniques and approaches described here for poetry are applicable to writing about novels, short stories, plays, and literary nonfiction.

To give you an idea of what a question paper looks like, read this poem by Emily Dickinson and the question paper that follows.

> I'm nobody! Who are you?
> Are you nobody, too?
> Then there's a pair of us—don't tell!
> They'd banish us, you know.
>
> How dreary to be somebody!
> How public, like a frog
> To tell your name the livelong day
> To an admiring bog!

Sample Student Question Paper

I wonder why she says she is nobody. I mean, she must have really low self-esteem or something. Does she mean that she's a nobody, nobody famous that is? Or does she feel bad about herself? Why does she ask if the reader feels like a nobody too? Why does she think this should be a secret? And why does she say it would be bad to be somebody? Doesn't everybody want to be somebody, if not somebody famous at least somebody who matters? It's weird how she says it would be dreary to be somebody. She makes it sound as though being somebody, say like Paris Hilton, would be awful because you'd spend all your time just being known. I mean, I'm kind of shy and wouldn't want to have my picture taken every time I went to the mall or bought a loaf of bread. What does this have to do with frogs, though? Maybe it's because frogs just make those croaking sounds all the time but nobody really listens. Or maybe she is saying that anybody who does listen to all that croaking is just a creature in the pond. Does this mean that the people who care about the famous and read about them in magazines are just wannabe somebodies, living through the lives of others? Is the writer saying it's better to be a nobody than someone who just keeps demanding attention from everyone around them?

Notice how the student seems to write her way into the beginnings of an interpretation of the poem. It is as though she couldn't help herself from attempting to answer her own questions.

Try It

Read this poem by Paul Laurence Dunbar (1872–1906) at least three times and then write about the poem for 10 minutes without stopping. Begin with questions but don't hesitate to take a stab at answering your own questions if ideas come to mind as you work. If you run out of things to write before the time is up, use one of these sentence starters to get you going again.

- "I wonder if . . ."
- "Could it be that . . . ?"
- "What if . . . ?"
- "Maybe the author was trying to say . . ."
- "It seems to me that . . ."
- "I suppose it's possible that . . ."

[TIP]

Before beginning to write your question paper, read the literary text you will be analyzing several times to make sure that you are familiar with both the content and the language.

We Wear The Mask
By Paul Laurence Dunbar

We wear the mask that grins and lies,
It hides our cheeks and shades our eyes,—
This debt we pay to human guile;
With torn and bleeding hearts we smile,
And mouth with myriad subtleties.

Why should the world be over-wise,
In counting all our tears and sighs?
Nay, let them only see us, while
    We wear the mask.

We smile, but, O great Christ, our cries
To thee from tortured souls arise.
We sing, but oh the clay is vile
Beneath our feet, and long the mile;
But let the world dream otherwise,
    We wear the mask!

_____

_____

_____

_____

_____

_____

_____

_____

_____

_____

_____

_____

_____

_____

_____

_____

_____

_____

_____

_____

_____

_____

_____

_____

_____

_____

_____

_____

_____

_____

_____

_____

Now read Paul Laurence Dunbar's poem "We Wear the Mask" again.

1. Do you feel you understand it better than you did before writing the question paper? Explain.

_____

_____

_____

2. How did this kind of free writing help you figure out what you do and don't understand about the poem?

_____

_____

_____

3. What else would you want to know before trying to write an analytical essay about this poem?

_____

_____

_____

[TIP]

Biographical information about authors is easy to find on the Internet, but be sure to consider the source when evaluating the quality of the information you find.

Biographical Information

Sometimes information about a poet can deepen your understanding of a poem. Read the following paragraphs about Emily Dickinson and Paul Laurence Dunbar and reflect on how this additional information influences your thinking about their poems.

Emily Dickinson (1830–1886) rarely left her family's house in Amherst, Massachusetts, except to go to church. Known almost as much for her reclusive life as for her enormous body of work, the Belle of Amherst broke all the traditional rules of poetry writing. Though the author of over 1,700 poems, only 10 were published in her lifetime and these were published without her permission. After Emily's death, her sister found and published a collection of the poems. The sudden success of this collection with readers is almost without parallel in American literature.

How does this biographical information add to or influence your understanding of "I'm nobody. Who are you?"

_____

_____

_____

_____

_____

_____

_____

_____

_____

_____

_____

_____

Paul Laurence Dunbar (1872–1906) was born in Dayton, Ohio, the son of former slaves. He began writing poetry at 12 years old, but it wasn't until his second volume of poetry *Majors and Minors* (1895) came to the attention of William Dean Howells that Dunbar's work began to be widely read. Dunbar was the first black writer in the United States to support himself by writing and the first to gain national prominence. In his writing Dunbar used two distinct voices—the standard English of the classical poet and the dialect of turn-of-the-century black country folks. Though he did not live to see it happen, his serious lyric poems have come to be critically acclaimed along with his artistic use of dialect. Paul Laurence Dunbar died of tuberculosis at the age of 33.

How does this biographical information add to or influence your understanding of "We Wear the Mask"?

_____

_____

_____

_____

_____

_____

_____

_____

_____

Reading Poetry

Poetry can be intimidating. Poets can pack so much meaning into so few words that readers are sometimes thoroughly puzzled by the text. Before proceeding to the next lesson where you will be selecting a poem to write an analytical essay about, review these guidelines for reading poetry.

1. Do not expect to understand the full meaning of a poem on a single, quick reading. The first time through you may only have a vague sense of what the poem is about. Read a poem multiple times before attempting to analyze it.

2. Do not assume that the "I" in the poem is always the poet. Sometimes poets write from the perspective of another person.

3. Look up words you don't know. In a poem every word is chosen with great care. Your understanding will be impaired if, for example, you don't know what a *bog* is in the Emily Dickinson poem.

4. Pay attention not only to WHAT is being said in the poem but also HOW it is being said. Is the language conversational or formal? Is the tone gloomy or cheerful? Knowing this can give you important insight into the meaning behind the poet's words.

5. When choosing a poem to analyze, pick one that appeals to you. You will be more invested in your analysis if you genuinely want to understand the poem better.

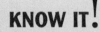 **KNOW IT!** Before you begin to analyze literature, make sure to explore your own understanding of the text thoroughly. Taking time to write about the questions the text raises in your mind can help you discover what to write about in your essay.

Think about the speed with which you do everyday things, such as tying your shoes or brushing your teeth. You are so used to doing these tasks that you probably rush through them, not paying much attention to the actual process involved. But when you do something less common or more complicated, such as cooking a new recipe or putting together a piece of furniture, you have to slow down and really pay attention to what's going on. In order to understand poetry well enough to write about it, you need to take the same kind of care as you read. For most of the reading you do in your daily life—newspapers, magazines, Web sites, brochures—you can read quickly and still understand everything you need to about the text. In order to write about literature, and particularly when analyzing poetry, you need to slow down your reading and really pay attention.

Because poems are so highly compressed and use such concentrated language, it can often help to paraphrase the poem before you try to interpret it. Work through the poem line by line, figuring out what is going on. If the poem is written in sentences, try to identify each subject and verb. Don't be surprised if it takes many more words to paraphrase a poem than it took the poet to write the original.

In addition to paraphrasing, another way to help you slow yourself down and make sure you pay attention to every word is to read with a pen or pencil in hand. Follow these guidelines for reading any poem you plan to analyze.

1. **During your first reading of the poem**, circle the words you don't fully understand and the expressions that aren't clear to you. Look up the words and try to figure out what the expressions might mean in the context of the poem. Often the expressions have more than one meaning!

2. **During your second reading of the poem**, underline phrases that seem to be important to the poem's meaning. Make notes on what these phrases suggest to you or make you think of. Try to interpret what the poet has written.

3. **After your third reading of the poem**, comment on what you think the poem says and how it makes you feel. Make personal connections to the poem.

Notice how paraphrasing and marking up the text helped this student interpret "I Wandered Lonely as a Cloud" by William Wordsworth.

[TIP]

As you mark up the poem, you might also want to draw arrows between connected ideas and write additional comments in the margins.

I Wandered Lonely as a Cloud
By William Wordsworth

I wandered <u>lonely as a cloud</u>
That floats on high (o'er vales) and hills,
When all at once I saw a crowd,
(A host, of golden daffodils;)
Beside the lake, beneath the trees,
Fluttering and <u>dancing in the breeze</u>.

<u>Continuous as the stars</u> that shine
And twinkle on (the milky way,)
They stretched in never-ending line
Along the margin of a bay:
Ten thousand saw I at a glance,
<u>Tossing their heads</u> in sprightly dance.

The waves beside them danced; but they
Out-did the sparkling waves (in glee:)
A poet could not but be gay,
In such a (jocund company:)
I gazed—and gazed—but little thought
<u>What wealth the show to me had brought</u>:

For oft, when on my couch I lie
In vacant or in pensive mood,
They flash upon (that inward eye)
Which is the bliss of solitude;
And then my heart with pleasure fills,
And dances with the daffodils.

Paraphrase of "I Wandered Lonely as a Cloud":

The speaker in the poem tells about a day when he was on a walk wandering through nature when suddenly he came upon a field of blooming daffodils. He was amazed by how many he could see in a glance. They seemed to be everywhere—near the water, under the trees—and he delighted in how the flowers bent and moved in the wind. It seemed as though they were dancing. As a poet he could not help but respond to the joyful display of spring flowers. He felt that the sight of these daffodils was a gift, a treasure. Now whenever he is feeling alone or depressed, he thinks back to those flowers and his mood improves as he remembers the beauty and surprise they brought him that day. His heart dances with the memory of the yellow flowers.

Notes from first reading (circled):

- *o'er vales:* over valleys
- *a host, of golden daffodils:* a huge number of blooming yellow flowers
- *the milky way:* a galaxy full of stars
- *in glee:* in delight, joyfully
- *jocund company:* happy, laughing friends
- *that inward eye:* his mind's eye, memory

Notes from second reading (underlined):

- *lonely as a cloud:* the speaker compares himself to a cloud floating above a spring landscape
- *dancing in the breeze:* the poet personifies the daffodils, comparing their movement in the wind to a dance
- *continuous as the stars:* like the stars, there are so many they seem uncountable
- *tossing their heads:* the personification continues to compare the blooms of the daffodils with the heads of happy dancers
- *what wealth the show to me had brought:* the poet reflects on the gift the sight of the daffodils gave him—riches for his spirit

Notes from third reading of the poem (personal connection):

The poet recalls a day when, walking along with his head in the clouds, he suddenly came upon a field of daffodils. Their number and beauty cause his mood to shift and his heart to be lifted. It was like when you are feeling depressed and suddenly see something so surprising and beautiful that it wakes you up out of yourself—like a sunset or a mountain or a pretty girl. The flowers take such delight in just being themselves that the poet thinks about the importance of the simple joys in life. Whatever he was worrying about seems forgotten. Whenever he is feeling lonely or depressed, he conjures up the image of these dancing daffodils in his mind and the memory of that day refreshes him. It is as though thinking about the flowers has the power lift his spirits. The poem seems to be about the healing power of nature to help get rid of a bad or sad mood.

[TIP]

Personification is a figure of speech in which animals, ideas, or inanimate objects are given human characteristics. For example, in "I Wandered Lonely as a Cloud," Wordsworth personifies the daffodils when he describes them "tossing their heads" and dancing.

For more information on **personification**, see p. 222.

Try It

It is now time for you to choose a poem as the subject for your essay. Read through the following poems and select one that appeals or intrigues you. Don't worry if you don't understand the poems at first. Working through the steps outlined in this lesson will help you figure it out.

A Poison Tree
By William Blake

I was angry with my friend:
I told my wrath, my wrath did end.
I was angry with my foe:
I told it not, my wrath did grow.

And I watered it in fears
Night and morning with my tears,
And I sunned it with smiles
And with soft deceitful wiles.

And it grew both day and night,
Till it bore an apple bright,
And my foe beheld it shine,
And he knew that it was mine,

And into my garden stole
When the night had veiled the pole;
In the morning, glad, I see
My foe outstretched beneath the tree.

The Debt
By Paul Laurence Dunbar

This is the debt I pay
Just for one riotous day,
Years of regret and grief,
Sorrow without relief.

Pay it I will to the end—
Until the grave, my friend,
Gives me a true release—
Gives me the clasp of peace.

Slight was the thing I bought,
Small was the debt I thought,
Poor was the loan at best—
God! but the interest!

How Do I Love Thee?
By Elizabeth Barrett Browning

How do I love thee? Let me count the ways.
I love thee to the depth and breadth and height
My soul can reach, when feeling out of sight
For the ends of being and ideal grace.
I love thee to the level of every day's
Most quiet need, by sun and candle-light.
I love thee freely, as men strive for right;
I love thee purely, as they turn from praise.
I love thee with the passion put to use

In my old griefs, and with my childhood's faith.
I love thee with a love I seemed to lose
With my lost saints. I love thee with the breath,
Smiles, tears, of all my life; and, if God choose,
I shall but love thee better after death.

Success
By Emily Dickinson

Success is counted sweetest
By those who ne'er succeed.
To comprehend a nectar
Requires sorest need.

Not one of all the purple host
Who took the flag to-day
Can tell the definition,
So clear, of victory,

As he, defeated, dying,
On whose forbidden ear
The distant strains of triumph
Break, agonized and clear!

Trees
By Joyce Kilmer

I think that I shall never see
A poem lovely as a tree.

A tree whose hungry mouth is prest
Against the earth's sweet flowing breast;

A tree that looks at God all day,
And lifts her leafy arms to pray;

A tree that may in Summer wear
A nest of robins in her hair;

Upon whose bosom snow has lain;
Who intimately lives with rain.

Poems are made by fools like me,
But only God can make a tree.

If....
By Rudyard Kipling

If you can keep your head when all about you
Are losing theirs and blaming it on you;
If you can trust yourself when all men doubt you,
But make allowance for their doubting too;
If you can wait and not be tired by waiting,
Or being lied about, don't deal in lies,
Or being hated, don't give way to hating,
And yet don't look too good, nor talk too wise:

If you can dream, and not make dreams your master;
If you can think, and not make thoughts your aim;
If you can meet with Triumph and Disaster
And treat those two imposters just the same;
If you can bear to hear the truth you've spoken
Twisted by knaves to make a trap for fools,
Or watch the things you gave your life to, broken,
And stoop and build 'em up with worn-out tools;

If you can make one heap of all your winnings
And risk it on one turn of pitch-and-toss,
And lose, and start again at your beginnings
And never breathe a word about your loss;
If you can force your heart and nerve and sinew
To serve your turn long after they are gone,
And so hold on when there is nothing in you
Except the Will which says to them: "Hold on!"

If you can talk with crowds and keep your virtue,
Or walk with kings, nor lose the common touch,
If neither foes nor loving friends can hurt you,
If all men count with you, but none too much;
If you can fill the unforgiving minute
With sixty seconds' worth of distance run,
Yours is the Earth and everything that's in it,
And, which is more, you'll be a Man, my son!

Once you have chosen the poem you plan to analyze, follow the close-reading steps that follow. If you need more room, use a separate piece of paper.

1. Paraphrase the poem.

_____

_____

_____

_____

_____

_____

_____

2. Circle words you don't understand and expressions that aren't clear to you. List the words below, and then look them up before proceeding to Step 3.

_____

_____

_____

_____

3. Underline phrases in the poem that seem important to the poem's meaning. On the lines below, copy these phrases and make notes on what these phrases suggest to you or make you think of. Try to interpret what the poet has written.

• **Phrase from the poem:**

_____

What this phrase suggests:

_____

_____

• **Phrase from the poem:**

_____

What this phrase suggests:

_____

_____

- **Phrase from the poem:**

  _____

  What this phrase suggests:

  _____

  _____

- **Phrase from the poem:**

  _____

  What this phrase suggests:

  _____

  _____

- **Phrase from the poem:**

  _____

  What this phrase suggests:

  _____

  _____

4. In the space below comment on what you think the poem says and how it makes you feel. Make personal connections to the poem.

   _____

   _____

   _____

   _____

   _____

   _____

   _____

   _____

   _____

   _____

KNOW IT! When reading literature, slow down your reading and mark up the text as you read. Before you can interpret or analyze a text, you need to be sure you understand what it says.

Have you ever felt like someone meant something different than what they were actually saying? This can happen several ways. A person's tone can tell you if "Thanks a lot!" is said in true gratitude or exasperated annoyance. If you say that someone "has a heart like a stone," chances are you don't actually mean their heart is hard to the touch. In life, there is often more to what someone is saying than the words they actually use. The same holds true of poetry. Poets carefully craft words, phrases, and expressions to pack the most meaning possible. You task in analyzing poetry is to unwrap the layers of meaning behind the words themselves.

In order to fully analyze a poem, you have to figure out if there is a deeper meaning behind the language used. One way to do this is to use a graphic organizer like the one that follows to help you understand the poem you have chosen to analyze. Begin by rereading the poem carefully and selecting individual lines to examine. Copy these lines into the first column. In the second column paraphrase the lines in your own words. In the third column, jot any connections to your own experience that the line suggests. What do the poet's words make you think of? Does the line remind you of anyone you know or have heard or thought about? In the fourth column consider what the line might mean in relation to the whole poem. What **inferences** can you draw? What is significant about the line? Why does it matter? As you move across the columns you will notice that you become increasingly analytical about what you have read. Ask yourself what the poem says, what it means, and why it matters.

EXAMPLE

Doctors
By Sara Teasdale

Every night I lie awake
And every day I lie abed
And hear the doctors, Pain and Death,
Conferring at my head.

They speak in scientific tones,
Professional and low,
One argues for a speedy cure,
The other, sure and slow.

To one so humble as myself
It should be matter for some pride
To have such noted fellows here,
Conferring at my side.

Lines from poem	Paraphrase (What it says)	Make Connections (What it means)	Draw Inferences (Why it matters)
"Every night I lie awake"	The speaker in the poem can't sleep.	She must be in too much pain to fall asleep.	As she lies awake she starts thinking about pain and death.
"they speak in scientific tones"	Pain and death are talking to one another about the speaker's condition.	Just like doctors pain and death are arguing about what is the best treatment for the patient	The speaker is probably wondering who is right, which doctor will prevail.
"one argues for a speedy cure"	This must refer to Death because death can happen quickly.	The speaker is wondering if she could die.	Sometimes pain can be so strong that death seems better than living.
"the other, sure and slow"	This must refer to suffering through the pain in order to be healed.	Maybe the speaker is thinking about how long she will have to endure the pain.	Pain seems certain that over time the patient will recover.

Another way to search for deeper meaning is to explore how the **elements of literature** combine to create a particular effect. Literary elements include **figurative language**, **imagery**, and **sound devices**.

The most common types of figures of speech are **similes** and **metaphors**.

- A simile is a comparison between two things using the words *like* or *as*. For example, if you say *Jason is as strong as an ox*, the underlying meaning is that Jason is physically strong and probably mentally tough and determined as well. The comparison helps you understand *how* strong Jason is much more than if you just said, "Jason is pretty strong."

- A metaphor is a comparison between two things without using a connecting word—you actually say that one thing *is* another. For example, a poem might say *Ana is an angel*. This likely doesn't mean that Ana is dead and visiting Earth in a ghostly form, but rather that she is caring, compassionate, and helpful.

Imagery is writing that specifically appeals to the five senses. In order to recreate their experience—to show rather than tell—poets use words that appeal to our senses. Poems rich in imagery invite readers to experience what the writer has seen, felt, heard, smelled, and tasted. A poem that uses winter imagery might make reference to "cold, wet fields" or "snowy, silent afternoons" to make readers feel like they are actually there. A poem that uses spring imagery might make reference to "the warmth of the sun on your cheeks" or "the chirping of baby chicks."

For more information on the **elements of literature**, including **similes, metaphors, rhythm, rhyme,** and **alliteration**, see p. 222.

Sound devices contribute to the pleasure of reading a poem. While it is not always possible to read a poem aloud, you need to get into the habit of hearing a poem inside your head, listening to its beat, and paying attention to the sounds the words make. Poets use sound devices like **rhythm**, **rhyme**, and **alliteration** to create mood and convey meaning.

- Rhythm is the beat you feel when reading a line of poetry. Notice how the rhythm of these lines from Alfred, Lord Tennyson's "The Charge of the Light Brigade" gives the feeling of galloping horses:

> Half a league, half a league,
> Half a league onward,

- Rhyme is the repetition of sounds at the end of a line. For example:
An apple a <u>day</u>
Keeps the doctor <u>away</u>.

- Alliteration is the repetition of initial consonant sounds in a word. It is important to note that it's the *sound* that matters, not the actual letter. For example, "<u>F</u>ee, <u>f</u>ie, <u>f</u>oe, <u>f</u>um" or "<u>K</u>ate <u>q</u>uickly <u>k</u>issed the <u>c</u>at" are both examples of alliteration.

Simply identifying figurative language, imagery, and sound devices isn't enough. You need to analyze *how* these aspects of the poem contribute to its meaning. To help you do this, ask yourself the following questions. They will help you interpret what you have read.

1. What does the title of the poem suggest to you?

2. Who is speaking, what is the speaker saying to whom, and why?

3. How would you describe the poet's word choice? Does the poet use words that are formal or informal? Are they descriptive and flowery or lean and tight? What effect does this have?

4. Do you notice any repetition in the poem? What do these words, phrases, or lines emphasize?

5. What does the imagery in the poem cause you to see, hear, feel, smell, or taste?

6. What examples of figurative language can be found in the poem?

7. What effect does the poet's use of figurative language have on you?

8. What important words or phrases seem to stand out to you? Why do you think they're important?

9. What sound devices are used? Do they affect your interpretation of the poem?

10. What seems to be the central purpose of the poem? Why do you think the poet wrote it?

EXAMPLE

Here is an example of how one student worked through her analysis of the elements of literature to explore their contribution to the meaning of the poem "Doctors."

[TIP]

Rhythm is created by carefully arranging the pattern of stressed and unstressed syllables.

Poem title	"Doctors"
Author	Sara Teasdale
1. What does the title of the poem suggest to you?	The poem will be about doctors, people who help others who are hurt.
2. Who is speaking, what is the speaker saying to whom, and why?	The poet herself seems to be speaking, or at least someone who is sick and in pain and stuck in bed. The speaker is explaining that her "doctors," Pain and Death, are talking about her fate—will she die quickly or continue suffering?
3. How would you describe the poet's word choice? Does the poet use words that are formal or informal? Are they descriptive and flowery or lean and tight? What effect does this have?	The poem has a calm feeling, which is kind of strange since the speaker might be dying. She says that she feels honored to have such honored doctors as Pain and Death discussing her case. The poem does not make it seem like the speaker is really suffering—she just calmly discusses the "doctors" who are talking about her. This makes it seem like she's not really going to die, that she's kind of accepted the fact that she's just going to slowly get better.
4. Do you notice any repetition in the poem? What do these words, phrases, or lines emphasize?	No, nothing seems to be repeated.
5. What does the imagery in the poem cause you to see, hear, feel, smell, or taste?	When the speaker describes herself "awake" and "abed," we get a picture of a sick person unable to sleep and in pain. Though the poet can hear the doctors arguing, she doesn't describe that in such a way that we can hear it.
6. What examples of figurative language can be found in the poem?	The speaker in the poem refers to Pain and Death as her doctors, personifying them.
7. What effect does the poet's use of figurative language have on you?	It makes it seem like we aren't in charge of our own fate—like these two other forces are deciding what's going to happen to her, and all she can do is lay there and listen.

8. What important words or phrases seem to stand out to you? Why do you think they're important?	The speaker compares the "speedy cure" (death) with "slow and steady" recovery through pain—this is interesting because it almost makes death sound more appealing than recovery through pain! Calling Pain and Death "noted fellows" demonstrates her respect for the power of both.
9. What sound devices are used? Do they affect your interpretation of the poem?	The second and fourth lines in both stanzas rhyme. The poem has a steady beat. This seems to reflect how the patient is feeling—calm, not anxious or agitated.
10. What seems to be the central purpose of the poem? Why do you think the poet wrote it?	The poet seems to be describing the sense of helplessness she feels about her situation. She is sick and bed-ridden, and she feels like she will either die or suffer through a long recovery, and it's not up to her which of those happens.

Notice how this student used her analysis to lead her to a working thesis statement and supporting points for an essay about the poem "Doctors."

Working Thesis Statement: *In her poem "Doctors," Sara Teasdale considers the options of a painful recovery and death for someone who is sick.*

First Key Supporting Point: *Explain how the speaker in the poem is reflecting upon her current situation.*

Second Key Supporting Point: *Compare the alternatives offered by the two "doctors," Pain and Death.*

Third Key Supporting Point: *Discuss the significance of her doctors seeming to have control over what happens, while she seems to be powerless.*

Try It

Use the poem you selected in Lesson 2 to complete these two graphic organizers. You will find your ideas for developing your analysis of the poem emerge as you work through each one. Each line that you work with will become a quotation that you can later comment on in your draft.

Line Analysis

Lines from poem	Paraphrase (What it says)	Make Connections (What it means)	Draw Inferences (Why it matters)

Elements of Literature Analysis

Poem title	
Author	
1. What does the title of the poem suggest to you?	
2. Who is speaking, what is the speaker saying to whom, and why?	
3. How would you describe the poet's word choice? Does the poet use words that are formal or informal? Are they descriptive and flowery or lean and tight? What effect does this have?	
4. Do you notice any repetition in the poem? What do these words, phrases, or lines emphasize?	
5. What does the imagery in the poem cause you to see, hear, feel, smell, or taste?	

6. What examples of figurative language can be found in the poem?	
7. What effect does the poet's use of figurative language have on you?	
8. What important words or phrases seem to stand out to you? Why do you think they're important?	
9. What sound devices are used? Do they affect your interpretation of the poem?	
10. What seems to be the central purpose of the poem? Why do you think the poet wrote it?	

Draft Your Essay

Use the material in your graphic organizers to draft an essay analyzing the poem you chose in lesson 2. Be careful to write about more than just your personal response to the poem—whether or not you "like it." You must explain *how* the elements of the poem contribute to its effectiveness. Comment on specific lines and language, analyzing how they affect your understanding of the poem. This commentary is the "meat" of your essay. Use references to specific lines in the poem to develop your interpretation.

_____
_____
_____
_____
_____
_____
_____
_____
_____
_____
_____
_____
_____
_____
_____
_____
_____
_____
_____
_____
_____
_____
_____
_____
_____

> **[TIP]**
>
> A useful verb to employ when writing about literature is *suggest.* It leaves you room to point out something you notice in a poem without committing yourself to saying exactly what that something means. For example, "The steady beat and regular rhyme in the poem 'Doctors' *suggests* that the patient is calmly considering the advice of her two doctors, Pain and Death."

[TIP]

Don't be afraid to write about aspects of your poem that continue to puzzle you.

_____

_____

_____

_____

_____

_____

_____

_____

_____

_____

_____

_____

_____

_____

_____

_____

_____

_____

_____

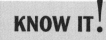

KNOW IT! When writing about poetry, you must analyze how the elements of literature (figurative language, imagery, and sound devices) contribute to the poem's meaning and effect. You should write about not only what the poem says, but also what it might mean on a deeper level.

Before moving to the next lesson, reread your poem and your draft, asking yourself the following questions:

- Have I provided readers with a clear statement of my thesis?
- Did I offer enough evidence from the poem to support my thesis?
- Did I analyze not only what the poem said, but what it meant?
- Did I evaluate the poet's use of figurative language and sound devices?
- Is my reader left with any unanswered questions?

If you feel as though your essay needs more work, now is the time to do it. Keep drafting until you feel you have analyzed your poem thoroughly. Don't be surprised if new insights about the poem occur to you as you write.

Did you find as you drafted your essay that you ran out of things to say? Do you sometimes wonder when you read another student's essay how the writer got from here to there, from poem to finished product? This lesson will demonstrate how one writer took the ideas in his graphic organizer and expanded them into a full essay.

When writing about literature a common problem is running out of things to say. You have the bare bones of your analysis charted in a graphic organizer but not enough material for a full essay. As a result, you may find you don't have enough supporting evidence. The key is to use the ideas in your graphic organizer as a springboard—those ideas should serve as the inspiration for a more detailed analysis.

The student used a graphic organizer like the one introduced in Lesson 3 to help him interpret individual lines from A. E. Housman's "To an Athlete Dying Young," making connections to what he knew and drawing inferences from this to explain why the individual lines were important to the poem's meaning.

EXAMPLE

To an Athlete Dying Young
By A. E. Housman

The time you won your town the race
We chaired you through the market-place;
Man and boy stood cheering by,
And home we brought you shoulder-high.

To-day, the road all runners come,
Shoulder-high we bring you home,
And set you at your threshold down,
Townsman of a stiller town.

Smart lad, to slip betimes away
From fields where glory does not stay,
And early though the laurel grows
It withers quicker than the rose.

Eyes the shady night has shut
Cannot see the record cut,
And silence sounds no worse than cheers
After earth has stopped the ears:

[TIP]

Always look up words you don't understand but also be on the lookout for words used in an unusual fashion. For example, "we chaired you" means that the athlete was carried by fans on a chair through the town to celebrate his victory.

Now you will not swell the rout
Of lads that wore their honours out,
Runners whom renown outran
And the name died before the man.

So set, before its echoes fade,
The fleet foot on the sill of shade,
And hold to the low lintel up
The still-defended challenge-cup.

And round that early-laurelled head
Will flock to gaze the strengthless dead,
And find unwithered on its curls
The garland briefer than a girl's.

Line Analysis

[TIP]

Remember that your goal is not a beautifully filled out graphic organizer but a fully developed essay. Use the graphic organizer as a tool to help you think about your poem.

Lines from poem	Paraphrase (What it says)	Make Connections (What it means)	Draw Inferences (Why it matters)
"Smart lad, to slip betimes away/From fields where glory does not stay"	The athlete was "smart" to die before his fame faded.	It seems odd to call dying a smart move.	The speaker seems to be reflecting on the fleeting nature of fame.
"And early though the laurel grows/ It withers quicker than the rose."	Laurel comes up early in the spring but it is not a long-lasting plant.	Laurel wreaths were used as a crown for winning athletes. Unlike a crown made of gold, this isn't something you can hold onto or save.	I think it matters because he is saying that this kind of triumph lasts for only a short while.
"Eyes the shady night has shut/ Cannot see the record cut" "Now you will not swell the rout/ Of lads that wore their honours out,/ Runners whom renown outran/ And the name died before the man."	When you're dead, you're not there to witness your records beaten or see your accomplishments topped. This athlete won't join the group of people who out-lived their fame.	These lines remind me of the saying "outlived your glory." I always feel bad for people who feel like the best times of their lives are behind them and now all they do is sit and think about the old days when they were on top of the world.	The speaker seems to be saying that it is better to go out on top than to linger and see your accomplishments bested.

Notice how working through these important lines in the A.E. Housman poem helped the writer develop and support his interpretation of the poem.

Wearing the Laurel Wreath

In the poem "To an Athlete Dying Young," A.E. Housman is writing a poem about the glory of youth and athletes. He seems to say that youth is beautiful and that to live past youth is to outlive the beauty. This idea is a common one for poets, from the deaths of young Greek heroes through Shakespeare to James Dean and Heath Ledger.

Notice how this idea grew out of the notes the student took in the graphic organizer on the lines referring to the laurel and the rose.

One way this theme is expressed is in the use of the laurel wreath as a symbol of achievement. The laurel, used to make a crown for athletes in the old days, is a very short-lived plant. Housman is saying that the fame the crown represents will soon fade. The image of the rose suggests beauty. Though longer lived than the laurel, roses also wither and die. If the athlete hadn't died young, not only would his records have been broken but also his youthful, beautiful appearance would have aged.

Housman is not just saying that the good die young. It seems hard to believe that he would take twenty-eight lines to express this idea. Instead, we should see the fourth and fifth stanzas as keys to the meaning of the poem. As athletes age, they not only see records broken, but they themselves become less important than their early achievements. In other words, their youthful achievements actually matter more than they do. They wear their honors out; fame outruns them; their names die before they do.

This observation about the relative benefits of dying young stem from the student's comments on the quotes about records cut and the name dying before the man.

Housman does not dwell on the fate of outliving your glory days though. This poem is not about the gloom of growing older. He focuses instead on the benefits of dying young, while you are still the best. It's better, he argues, to go out early but while on top than to live a long time but see all your accomplishments bested over time.

See how the student found ideas for the conclusion from observations about "fields where glory does not stay."

In the end, Housman is warning young men against becoming over-impressed with their athletic achievements. The fortunate are those who die while their glory is intact. Those that outlive that glory—and eventually see it lost—are less worthy; they wear their honors out.

■ Try It

On the following page is a rubric for effective literary analysis essays. Use it and the questions that follow to evaluate the student essay "Wearing the Laurel Wreath."

LITERARY ANALYSIS WRITING RUBRIC (5-point scale)

A **5 literary analysis essay** offers an insightful interpretation of a piece of literature. The writer explains the text thoroughly, making a compelling case in support of its thesis. The essay is focused, demonstrates a clear sense of purpose and audience, and uses appropriate tone and style. Organization is coherent with appropriate transitions between and within paragraphs to create a cohesive whole. Word choice is precise, sentences are varied, and grammatical errors are rare or absent.

A **4 literary analysis essay** presents a competent interpretation of a piece of literature. The writer explains the text coherently and with appropriate supporting evidence. The essay generally maintains its focus and demonstrates a sense of purpose, tone, and audience. Organization is generally clear with transitions between paragraphs. A competency with language is apparent. Word choice is appropriate and sentences are sometimes varied. Some errors in sentence structure, usage, and mechanics are present.

A **3 literary analysis essay** presents a minimally competent interpretation of the piece of literature. The writer offers some commentary on the significance of supporting evidence, but the essay lacks analysis and may consist largely of unexplained quotations. The essay generally maintains its focus with minor digressions. Its sense of purpose, tone, and audience may be unclear. Organization is clear enough to follow. A limited control of language is apparent. Word choice is imprecise and sentences may be poorly constructed or confusing. Errors in sentence structure, usage, and mechanics are present.

A **2 literary analysis essay** presents a weakly developed interpretation of a piece of literature. The writer offers minimal and/or inappropriate commentary to connect quotations to the essay's thesis. The essay demonstrates significant problems in one or more of the following areas, which makes the writer's ideas difficult to follow: unclear focus, lack of organization, weak controlling idea, and redundancy. Style and tone may be inappropriate for the audience. Writing demonstrates weak control of language. A pattern of errors in grammar and mechanics significantly interferes with meaning.

A **1 literary analysis essay** presents an ineffective interpretation of a piece of literature. Ideas and commentary are absent, irrelevant, unsupported by evidence, or incomprehensible. The essay lacks focus and organization, making the writer's ideas difficult to follow. Style and tone may be inappropriate for the audience. Writing demonstrates poor control of language. Errors in grammar and mechanics are pervasive and obstruct meaning.

For each of the following questions, circle the option that best describes the student's essay, "Wearing the Laurel Wreath." Explain your answer on the lines that follow.

1. Is the writer's interpretation:

   - insightful? (makes unique, creative discoveries about the deeper meaning of the text)
   - adequate? (just enough to help readers understand the deeper meaning of the text)
   - inadequate? (does not explore deeply enough the meaning of the text)

   Explain your answer using examples from the essay.

   _____

   _____

   _____

   _____

   _____

2. Is the essay:

   - clearly focused and carefully organized?
   - somewhat focused with some off-topic discussion?
   - disorganized?

   Explain your answer using examples from the essay.

   _____

   _____

   _____

   _____

   _____

3. Is the essay:

   - free from distracting grammatical and mechanical errors?
   - mostly free from grammatical and mechanical errors?
   - full of distracting grammatical and mechanical errors?

   Explain your answer using examples from the essay.

   _____

   _____

   _____

   _____

   _____

4. Is the essay:

- written in an appropriate style and voice and a pleasure to read?
- well written with a few awkward places?
- poorly written in a conversational tone?

Explain your answer using examples from the essay.

_____

_____

_____

_____

5. Based on the rubric, what score would you assign to this essay? ____

Explain why you think this score is appropriate for this essay. Offer the writer suggestions for improving his essay.

_____

_____

_____

_____

_____

_____

_____

_____

_____

_____

_____

_____

_____

[TIP]

Borrow language from the scoring guide in your explanation to the student writer. Try to be encouraging. Suggest places in the poem that need further analysis. Let the writer know what he has done well along with what he might do better.

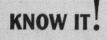

KNOW IT! Evaluating another student's writing can help you evaluate your own work. Use the Literary Analysis Writing Rubric to help you determine what you need to do to improve your draft and write an excellent literary response essay.

Do you enjoy rearranging the furniture in your apartment? When dressing for a party, do you like to try out pieces from your wardrobe in new combinations to create a more interesting outfit? Do you find yourself revising a recipe as you cook? All of these instincts for improvement can be put to good use when revising an essay.

Now that you have your analysis of your poem down on paper, it's time to work on polishing your writing. Literary analysis should be written in a formal tone that convinces readers that you know what you are talking about. To accomplish this you will want to make sure that your revised essay:

- clearly explains the poem you have chosen to analyze.

- uses lines from the poem to support your analysis.

- comments on those lines in detail, describing how particular word choices contribute to the poem's meaning.

- reflects upon the significance of the ideas in the poem.

- develops each supporting point fully.

- uses appropriate language and tone.

Using appropriate language and tone in your essay means replacing conversational, informal expressions with the language of literary analysis. Along with lending credibility to your argument by making your essay sound like the work of someone who knows what he or she is talking about, revising the language in your draft helps you express your ideas more clearly. It isn't a matter of replacing short words with long ones but rather revising vague, general terms like *good*, *bad*, *interesting*, *a lot*, *thing*, *stuff*, and *different* with sharper, more precise words. Writing about literature is actually easier when you have a large vocabulary to work with. Most students know more many more words than they typically use in their writing. The challenge—and one of the goals of this lesson—is to get into the habit of using those words when you put pen to paper.

EXAMPLE

Here are suggestions of precise vocabulary to use as you revise your draft:

Useful verbs for writing about literature

- *Try replacing the verb in "the poem says" or "the line means" with:*

expresses	invites
suggests	develops
explores	depicts

Useful adjectives for praising a writer's style

- *Try replacing "interesting" or "exciting" with:*

appealing	complex
attention-grabbing	electrifying
exhilarating	precise
fascinating	remarkable
moving	stirring

Useful adjectives for criticizing a writer's style

- *Try replacing "bad" or "boring" with:*

dreadful	long-winded
dreary	mind-numbing
dull	tiresome
ghastly	wearisome

Useful adjectives for describing the mood of a poem

anxious	peaceful
cheerful	playful
eerie	soothing
haunting	tense
lonely	

Take a look at the following weak sentences, which have been revised using more precise language. The sentences refer to the A. E. Housman poem from Lesson 4. Circle the new and improved language in each revised sentence.

- **Weak sentence:** In the poem "To an Athlete Dying Young," A.E. Housman says that it is good to die before your fame is gone.

  Revised sentence: In the poem "To an Athlete Dying Young," A.E. Housman explores the idea that it is preferable to die young, before one's fame has faded.

- **Weak sentence:** The line "Townsman of a stiller town" means that the winning athlete is now dead and in a graveyard.

  Revised sentence: Calling the dead athlete a "Townsman of a stiller town" refers to the fact that he now resides in a graveyard.

- **Weak sentence:** In the third stanza the poet says that now that the athlete is dead, his eyes are shut so he can't see his records broken, and his ears are stopped so he can't hear that no one is cheering any more.

  Revised sentence: In the third stanza the poet uses visual and auditory imagery to convey how the dead athlete can no longer see his records broken or hear that the cheering has stopped.

To develop the habit of replacing weak words with stronger language, revise the following paragraph using more precise language. Include concrete details from the poem to develop this bare-bones paragraph more fully.

The mood of A.E. Housman's poem "To An Athlete Dying Young" is sad but also hopeful. You can see this by the words he uses. Poems about death are always sad. The celebration at the beginning of the poem is a happy moment in the athlete's life which ends soon after. This is a poem about the things that happen when someone dies young.

_____

_____

_____

_____

_____

_____

_____

[TIP]

The more you practice using precise words, the more natural writing in a formal tone will become for you.

Sample revision

For a poem addressed to a dead man, the mood of this poem is surprisingly upbeat and hopeful, suggesting that the young athlete will be remembered in his glory. We see evidence of this mood in the lines, "Man and boy stood cheering by/And home we brought you shoulder-high." The whole town is celebrating the athlete's victory. In the second stanza the mood becomes more somber as the friends carry the athlete's coffin shoulder high, but the speaker in the poem goes on to describe how the athlete's glory will survive him. This is said not sorrowfully but as a kind of consolation to the young man who has died. This poem reflects upon the bittersweet nature of dying in the prime of one's life.

▪ Try It

Reread your draft, circling any words that you think are vague or weak. Use the lists above and/or a thesaurus to find more precise words to substitute for your original choices.

Did you notice particular words that you used over and over again, words like *really* and *very*?

Add to the chart below to create a list of words that you overuse; be sure to include suggestions for replacements.

Tired, weak, or overused words	Possible replacements
really	in fact, in truth, certainly, truly
very	incredibly, vastly, enormously
a lot	plenty, many, a great number

Use the following chart to help you revise your draft. Ask yourself the questions in the first column and then follow the directions indicated in the second column. Record any changes you make to your draft in the third column.

Questions	Do this	Changes to your draft
1. Does your introduction engage a reader's interest in your analysis?	Think of a way to interest a reader in your poem.	
2. Have you included the author's name and the title of the poem in your opening paragraph?	Insert the author's name and title of the poem if you have omitted them.	
3. Are your supporting points clearly stated?	Underline the topic sentence in each supporting paragraph.	
4. Does every supporting paragraph include evidence from the poem?	Highlight all quoted lines from the poem. Make sure they are surrounded with quotation marks.	
5. Is every quotation accompanied by commentary?	Make sure each supporting paragraph is well-developed and includes a restatement and explanation for every quotation.	
6. Does the essay include transition words that guide the reader from point to point in the essay?	Circle transitional words and phrases.	
7. Do you restate your thesis in your conclusion?	Discuss the significance of your thesis in your conclusion.	

KNOW IT! In order to write well, all writers must revise their work. Paying careful attention to the words you use will help your literary analysis have a formal tone and persuade readers that you know what you are writing about.

Eliminating mechanical errors is a bit like scrubbing the floor. Wouldn't it be easier if someone else could just clean up the mess? Unfortunately there seldom seems to be someone around when you need it most. This lesson will help you be on the lookout for the most common errors in writing and, over time, help you to stop making them in the first place.

Though the rules of English grammar are many and occasionally very confusing, most of the errors that writers make fall into a short list.

The Most Common Errors in Student Writing:

1. Wrong word

2. Missing comma after an introductory phrase

3. Incomplete or missing citation of research

4. Unclear pronoun reference

5. Spelling

6. Punctuation or capitalization errors with a quotation

7. Unnecessary comma

8. Unnecessary or missing capitalization

9. Missing word

10. Unnecessary shift in verb tense

11. Missing comma in a compound sentence

12. Unnecessary or missing apostrophe

13. Run-on sentence

14. Sentence fragment

15. Lack of pronoun-antecedent agreement

Many of these mechanical errors, like run-ons and fragments (Unit 1), citing sources (Unit 2), problems with pronouns (Unit 3), and commonly confused words (Unit 4) have been addressed in previous units. This lesson will focus one of the remaining common errors on the list: the use and misuse of commas.

There are many rules that govern comma usage in the English language. However, if you can master the five rules that follow, you will know how to correctly use commas 95% of the time.

1. Use a comma between two independent clauses that are joined by *for, and, nor but, or, yet,* or *so.*

   Example: Marta ran all the way to the market, but she didn't make it before the store closed.

2. Use a comma to set off **appositives**. Appositives are explanatory words or phrases that add extra information about a noun or pronoun.

   Example: The two friends, former high school sweethearts, talked about old times.

3. Use commas between items in a series.

   Example: John wanted new shoes, a new watch, or tickets to a baseball game for his birthday.

4. Use a comma after an introductory phrase.

   Example: With a guilty look in his eye, Dmitri confessed that he was escaping the new baby's crying.

For more **comma usage** rules, see p. 219.

5. Use commas to separate adverbs such as *however, nevertheless,* and *instead,* and transitional phrases such as *for example, in fact, as a result,* and *in conclusion* from the rest of the sentence.

   Example: I really want to help you; however, circumstances make it impossible. In fact, I have tried to help you many times in the past.

EXAMPLE

Read the following sentences carefully, inserting commas where necessary. If the sentence is correct as is, mark it with a "C."

1. Mark my best friend is coming to pick me up.

2. Convinced she was right, Mandy kept arguing her point.

[TIP]

To remember the seven coordinating conjunctions, think of the acronym FANBOYS (For, And, Nor, But, Or, Yet, So).

3. Without any interference from Tom it was easy to install the new television.

4. I carried the heavy box up the stairs and lifted it onto the shelf.

5. When Julia arrived home she was delighted to see that dinner was already on the table.

6. My father Henry Charles Lewis is the head of our family.

7. Jody went to the pharmacy but forgot to buy cough drops nasal spray and tissue.

8. I'm trying to remember your name but I have a terrible memory.

9. Sarah likes fashion magazines; in fact, she loves them!

10. Marcy asked him about his family questioned him about his job and told him about her new puppy.

Correct Answers for comma practice

1. Mark, my best friend, is coming to pick me up. (*Use commas to set off appositives.*)

2. Correct as is. (*Use a comma after an introductory phrase.*)

3. Without any interference from Tom, it was easy to install the new television. (*Use comma after an introductory phrase.*)

4. Correct as is. (*Sentence does not contain two independent clauses.*)

5. When Julia arrived home, she was delighted to see that dinner was already on the table. (*Use comma after an introductory phrase.*)

6. My father, Henry Charles Lewis, is the head of our family. (*Use commas to set off appositives.*)

7. Jody went to the pharmacy but forgot to buy cough drops, nasal spray, and tissue. (*Use commas to separate items in a series.*)

8. I'm trying to remember your name, but I have a terrible memory. (*Use a comma to separate two independent clauses joined by a coordinating conjunction.*)

9. Correct as is. (*Use a comma to separate transitional phrases from the rest of the sentence.*)

10. Marcy asked him about his family, questioned him about his job, and told him about her new puppy. (*Use commas to separate items in a series.*)

[TIP]

Spelling used to be the most common mistake, but with so many people writing on computers and trusting that spell-check knows better than they do, "wrong word" has become the most common error.

The following student essay analyzes the Emily Dickinson poem "I'm Nobody! Who are you?" from Lesson 1 in this unit. The draft contains many of the common errors described at the beginning of this lesson, not only comma errors. Read and edit this essay, correcting the mistakes using the common editing marks found on page 231. Then check your edits against the revised essay.

I'm Nobody, Too

In her poem "I'm Nobody! Who are you?" Emily Dickinson explores the idea that it is better to be private and quiet then loud and famous. She begins by asking readers to consider weather or not they are "nobodies." This friendly invitation establishes the engaging tone of the poem, and makes readers want to know more about why the speaker in the poem calls herself a "nobody."

In the first stanza the speaker warns the reader not to tell anyone about they're being nobodies because, "They'd banish us, you know." This line suggests that people who don't assert theirselves publicly get pushed to the sidelines and away from the action. It seems as though Dickinson is saying that people who are somebody famous people don't like having nobodies around, maybe because they simply take up space in the room.

In the second stanza Dickinson criticized people who think they are important. She compares them to stupid frogs croking their names all day long "To an admiring bog!" This powerful image of a frog suggesting not only the slimy loathsome nature of the creature but also the pointlessness of everything that comes out of its mouth causes the reader to want to identify him or herself with the speaker, a "nobody."

In conclusion this Emily Dickinson poem is a delightful commentary comparing loud-mouthed extroverts with shy introverts. The poet makes it clear whom she prefers to be around.

Corrected Student Essay

I'm Nobody, Too

In her poem "I'm Nobody! Who are you?" Emily Dickinson

wrong word — explores the idea that it is better to be private and quiet ~~then~~ *than* loud and

wrong word — famous. She begins by asking readers to consider ~~weather~~ *whether* or not they are

"nobodies." This friendly invitation establishes the engaging tone of the

no comma needed here, compound verb, not a compound sentence — poem~~,~~ and makes readers want to know more about why the speaker in the

poem calls herself a "nobody."

In the first stanza the speaker warns the reader not to tell anyone

wrong word — about ~~they're~~ *their* being nobodies because, "They'd banish us, you know." This

wrong word — line suggests that people who don't assert ~~theirselves~~ *themselves* publicly get pushed

to the sidelines and away from the action. It seems as though Dickinson

insert two commas to set off appositive — is saying that people who are somebody, famous people, don't like having

nobodies around, maybe because they simply take up space in the room.

keep verbs in the present tense throughout essay — In the second stanza Dickinson ~~criticized~~ *criticizes* people who think they are

spelling — important. She compares them to stupid frogs cro*a*king their names all day

long "To an admiring bog!" This powerful image of a frog, suggesting not

insert two commas to set off appositive — only the slimy loathsome nature of the creature but also the pointlessness

of everything that comes out of its mouth, causes the reader to want to

identify him or herself with the speaker, a "nobody."

insert comma after introductory transitional phrase — In conclusion, this Emily Dickinson poem is a delightful

commentary comparing loud-mouthed extroverts with shy introverts. The

poet makes it clear whom she prefers to be around.

Try It

Employing the same editing skills you practiced on this sample student essay, edit the draft of your literary analysis essay. Pay careful attention to the most common errors in student writing. To help you identify which errors you make the most, keep a tally of the corrections you make to your draft.

Common Error	Tally of how many times you corrected this error in your draft
1. Wrong word	
2. Missing comma after an introductory phrase	
3. Incomplete or missing citation of research	
4. Unclear pronoun reference	
5. Spelling	
6. Punctuation or capitalization errors with a quotation	
7. Unnecessary comma	
8. Unnecessary or missing capitalization	
9. Missing word	
10. Unnecessary shift in verb tense	
11. Missing comma in a compound sentence	
12. Unnecessary or missing apostrophe	
13. Run-on sentence	
14. Sentence fragment	
15. Lack of pronoun-antecedent agreement	

KNOW IT! Learning about commonly made errors can help you correct these mistakes in your writing. By focusing on the *reason* for each correction, you will—over time—stop making these mistakes in the first place!

Wrap It Up

Use the rubric below (introduced in lesson 5.4) to evaluate your essay before you handing it in.

LITERARY ANALYSIS WRITING RUBRIC (5-point scale)

A 5 literary analysis essay offers an insightful interpretation of a piece of literature. The writer explains the text thoroughly, making a compelling case in support of its thesis. The essay is focused, demonstrates a clear sense of purpose and audience, and uses appropriate tone and style. Organization is coherent with appropriate transitions between and within paragraphs to create a cohesive whole. Word choice is precise, sentences are varied, and grammatical errors are rare or absent.

A 4 literary analysis essay presents a competent interpretation of a piece of literature. The writer explains the text coherently and with appropriate supporting evidence. The essay generally maintains its focus and demonstrates a sense of purpose, tone, and audience. Organization is generally clear with transitions between paragraphs. A competency with language is apparent. Word choice is appropriate and sentences are sometimes varied. Some errors in sentence structure, usage, and mechanics are present.

A 3 literary analysis essay presents a minimally competent interpretation of the piece of literature. The writer offers some commentary on the significance of supporting evidence, but the essay lacks analysis and may consist largely of unexplained quotations. The essay generally maintains its focus with minor digressions. Its sense of purpose, tone, and audience may be unclear. Organization is clear enough to follow. A limited control of language is apparent. Word choice is imprecise and sentences may be poorly constructed or confusing. Errors in sentence structure, usage, and mechanics are present.

A 2 literary analysis essay presents a weakly developed interpretation of a piece of literature. The writer offers minimal and/or inappropriate commentary to connect quotations to the essay's thesis. The essay demonstrates significant problems in one or more of the following areas, which makes the writer's ideas difficult to follow: unclear focus, lack of organization, weak controlling idea, and redundancy. Style and tone may be inappropriate for the audience. Writing demonstrates weak control of language. A pattern of errors in grammar and mechanics significantly interferes with meaning.

A 1 literary analysis essay presents an ineffective interpretation of a piece of literature. Ideas and commentary are absent, irrelevant, unsupported by evidence, or incomprehensible. The essay lacks focus and organization, making the writer's ideas difficult to follow. Style and tone may be inappropriate for the audience. Writing demonstrates poor control of language. Errors in grammar and mechanics are pervasive and obstruct meaning.

My paper should score a: _____

Before completing this unit, pause for 10–15 minutes to reflect upon what you have learned about writing about literature. On the lines below discuss how you feel about your finished product.

Are you satisfied with what you have written? Why or why not?

_____

_____

_____

_____

_____

_____

_____

What aspects of writing about literature do you continue to struggle with? What do you feel you do well?

_____

_____

_____

_____

_____

_____

_____

What do you want to remember for the next time you have to write in this manner?

_____

_____

_____

_____

_____

_____

_____

_____

Student Tips for Success

• Get organized

Buy a calendar and keep track of all class meetings, due dates, and scheduled tests. Plan ahead to make sure that you have enough time to study for exams and to write your papers. Pulling "all-nighters" may sound like fun, but you rarely do your best work under such conditions.

• Don't miss class

No one will be taking attendance, but you need to be there. The easiest way to fall behind is to skip class. Borrowing someone else's notes is never the same as hearing the material first hand. If you have trouble getting up early or have a long way to drive to get to campus, try not to schedule 8 A.M. classes. If possible, arrive early so that you can sit up front and center and be settled into your desk before class begins. Though you may not like sitting in front, it will help you pay closer attention to what is being taught.

• Take advantage of all the help offered

Most campuses have writing tutors available for free! Don't be shy. Smart students get all the help they can. Writing tutors can help with planning and drafting an essay as well as proofreading it for errors. Find out where the writing lab is on campus and make stopping in before or after class a habit. Don't wait until the day before a test or the day before a paper is due to ask for help. And don't feel guilty about needing the help. Your tuition pays for this assistance, so take advantage of it!

• Get to know your professors

College instructors all keep office hours. Early in the semester, make an appointment to introduce yourself to your professors. The better you know one another, the easier it will be to ask for help when you need it. Many professors complain that students never come to see them. Bring a problem you are having trouble with or a draft of your essay to your appointment. It will help jump start your conversation.

- ## Listen first, take notes second

  Don't worry about writing down every word a professor says. It is more important to understand the content of the lesson and just jot down important ideas. Many professors provide their lecture notes online.

- ## Don't be intimidated

  Though the material is challenging, have confidence that with hard work and help you can succeed. Don't be afraid to ask a question in class. Chances are that many students sitting around you have the same question. Posing questions can help to clarify your thinking.

- ## Make friends in class to study with

  Study groups are a natural part of the college experience. Working with other students who are enrolled in class with you is an excellent way to cement your own understanding of the material. What you don't know, others will. What they don't know, you might. Edit and proofread each other's papers and get together before exams to review the material.

- ## Find quiet places to work

  It may be that you need to make the college library your second home. You need peace and quiet to learn. Find a spot that feels comfortable and get into the habit of scheduling time every day to prepare for class or to work on your writing.

- ## Manage your time

  Spending 3–4 hours a day in class may not seem like much, but remember that your time out of class is not necessarily "free time." You are expected to do most of your classwork out of class. Expect to spend one to two hours working independently outside of class for every hour that you spend in class.

Grammar Handbook

The following guidelines will help you avoid common errors in grammar, mechanics, and usage in your writing.

Fragments

Sentences must have a subject and a verb and be a complete thought capable of standing alone. If a sentence lacks a subject or a verb or is not a complete thought, it is a fragment.

> **Examples:** Eating bananas. (no main verb)
>
> Good for your health. (no subject or verb)
>
> Because they contain potassium. (not a complete thought)

Run-Ons

A run-on sentence occurs when two sentences are written as though they were a single sentence.

> **Example:** Eating bananas is good for your health they contain potassium.

This run-on can be corrected in one of three basic ways:

1. By inserting a period between the two sentences
   Example: Eating bananas is good for your health. They contain potassium.

2. By inserting a semicolon between the two sentences (note: this should only be done when the two sentences are closely related to each other)
   Example: Eating bananas is good for your health; they contain potassium.

3. By using a comma before a coordinating conjunction between the two sentences
   Example: Eating bananas is good for your health, and they contain potassium.

You can also rewrite a run-on to change one of the complete sentences into a dependent clause.

> **Example:** Eating bananas is good for your health because they contain potassium.

A comma splice is a type of run-on sentence in which two complete thoughts are connected with just a comma. You can correct a comma splice by adding a coordinating conjunction after it, as seen in #3 above.

Types of Sentences

Most sentences fall into one of four categories.

1. Simple sentences are made up of a single independent clause. They may include a compound subject or compound verb.
   Examples: Tony eats apples.

   Tony and Terry eat apples and oranges.

2. Compound sentences are made up of two or more independent clauses joined with a comma and conjunction or with a semicolon.
   Examples: I eat apples, and Tony eats oranges.

   My lunch was great; I had a sandwich and apple.

3. **Complex sentences** include one independent clause and one or more dependent clauses.

    Examples: Although I love to eat, I'm careful about calories.

                  Because I don't eat meat and since I exercise, it's easy to keep my weight down.

4. **Compound-Complex sentences** are sentences that have two or more independent clauses and at least one dependent clause.

    Example: My friends and I went to a karaoke bar, but I didn't get on stage since I can't sing very well.

Conjunctions

Conjunctions link words, phrases, or clauses. There are three types of conjunctions:

1. **Coordinating conjunctions** join single words or groups of words, but they must always join similar elements, for example subject with subject, verb phrase with verb phrase, sentence with sentence. The seven coordinating conjunctions are *for, and, nor, but, or, yet,* and *so.* Remember to use a comma before coordinating conjunctions to connect two complete sentences.

2. **Correlative conjunctions** also connect sentence elements of the same kind, but they are always used in pairs. There is no need for special punctuation when using correlative conjunctions. The most commonly used are:

    • *both . . . and*

    • *not only . . . but also*

    • *either . . . or*

    • *neither . . . nor*

    • *whether . . . or*

3. **Subordinating conjunctions** connect subordinate, or dependent, clauses to a main clause, indicating the clause's relationship to the main clause. Examples of subordinating conjunctions are:

    • Cause and effect: *because, since, as, in order that, so*

    • Time: *before, after, when, while, until, since*

    • Opposition: *although, though, while, even though*

    • Condition: *if, whether, unless*

Note: if you use a subordinating conjunction at the beginning of a sentence, you must use a comma after the subordinate clause. If your subordinate clause comes as the last part of the sentence, you do not need to use a comma.

Examples: If it's hot enough, we'll go to the pool.

              We'll go to the pool if it's hot enough.

Commas

1. Use a comma between two independent clauses that are joined by a coordinating conjunction (*for, and, nor, but, or, yet,* or *so*).

    Examples: Jonas likes to eat hot dogs, but he knows they aren't good for him.

                Anna is a great cook, so her children eat very well.

2. Use commas to set off appositives. Appositives are explanatory words or phrases that rename or give more information about a noun or pronoun.

Examples: My car, an old Volvo, still runs well after 20 years on the road.

Joseph was looking for Lynne, the love of his life.

3. Use commas between items in a series.

Examples: Joan added peanut butter, jelly, and milk to her shopping list.

Madeline loves swimming in the pool, running in the park, and whistling in the dark.

4. Use a comma after an introductory phrase.

Examples: Worried about keeping his job, Bob worked extra hours.

Because he got a raise, Jose decided to buy a new car.

5. Use a comma after interjections such as *Yes, No,* and *Even so*.

Example: Yes, I'm sure I can help you change the tire.

6. Use a comma to separate adverbs, such as *however, nevertheless,* and *instead,* and transitional phrases, such as *for example, in fact,* and *as a result,* from the rest of the sentence.

Examples: I need you badly; however, you make it hard for me to keep you here.

In fact, I know Stephen can do the job.

7. When using quotations, place the exact words of the speaker inside quotation marks and set off the quotation from the rest of the sentence with a comma.

Examples: "I've told you not to wake me so early," Peter shouted.

Alex asked, "Why can't I come with you?"

"I'm not going," Julie said, "and you can't make me!"

8. Use a comma between a city and state and between elements of an address.

Examples: Anna has moved to Porterville, Virginia.

The company's new address is 1534 W. Antioch Street, Pacific Palisades, CA 90272.

9. Use commas to separate elements in a date.

Examples: My birthday is March 15, 1986.

July 4, 1776, is celebrated as Independence Day in the United States.

Pronouns

A pronoun is a part of speech that replaces nouns or other pronouns. Personal pronouns refer to specific people or things and change their form in order to agree with the nouns they represent, which are called antecedents. Make sure that every pronoun agrees in number, gender, and person with its antecedent.

Number: singular or plural, for example *I* or *we, he* or *they*.

Gender: masculine, feminine, or neuter, for example *he, she,* or *it*

Person: first person (I, we), second person (you), third person (he, she, they)

It is also important to use the correct case. There are three cases in English:

1. Subjective: used for the subject of a sentence or clause
   Examples: She broke her ankle.
   Who is coming to the movies?

2. Objective: used as the direct object of the verb or the object of the preposition.
   Examples: Jackie likes her very much. (direct object of verb *likes*)
   Maria couldn't see a foot in front of her. (object of the preposition *of*)
   For whom did you buy that bracelet? (object of the preposition *for*)

3. Possessive: used to indicate ownership
   Example: Her jacket was very expensive.

Reflexive pronouns are used when the object of a sentence is the same as the subject, as in "She hurt herself;" when the object of a preposition refers to the subject, as in "She was talking to herself when it happened;" and for emphasis, as in "She did it herself."

Each of the following pronouns takes a singular verb: *each, either, everyone, everybody, neither, nobody,* and *someone.*
   Example: Everyone needs to wear a coat on such a chilly day.

One of the most common pronoun errors is the incorrect use of *me* and *I* in compound constructions. Use the same case for the pronoun in a compound construction that you would if the pronoun were used alone.
   Examples: My friends and I are going to the movies. (ignore "My friends and")
   Timo is riding in the car with Janet and me. (ignore "Janet and")

Number	Person	Gender	Pronouns				
			subject	object	possessive	reflexive	possessive adjectives
	1st	m/f	I	me	mine	myself	my
	2nd	m/f	you	you	yours	yourself	your
singular		m	he	him	his	himself	his
	3rd	f	she	her	hers	herself	her
		n	it	it	its	itself	its
	1st	m/f	we	us	ours	ourselves	our
plural	2nd	m/f	you	you	yours	yourselves	your
	3rd	m/f/n	they	them	theirs	themselves	their

Subject/Verb Agreement

1. Subjects and verbs in a sentence must agree in number. Both must be singular or plural.
   Examples: The <u>dogs</u> in the village <u>are</u> mostly strays.

   <u>A cup</u> of coffee <u>is</u> the perfect morning beverage.

2. If the subject of a sentence is made up of two or more nouns connected by *and,* use a plural verb.
   Example: <u>Mary and Jack are</u> going to the mall together.

3. When two or more singular nouns are connected by *or* or *nor,* use a singular verb.
   Example: Either <u>apple or orange juice is</u> fine with me.

4. When a compound subject contains both a singular and a plural noun or pronoun joined by *or* or *nor,* the verb should agree with the part of the subject that is closest to the verb.
   Examples: Neither John nor <u>his friends like</u> that book.

   Either the cats or <u>their owner is</u> going to have to move out.

5. Don't be confused by a phrase that comes between the subject and the verb. The verb agrees with the subject, not with a noun or pronoun in the phrase.
   Example: <u>One</u> of my friends <u>is</u> free tonight.

Literary Terminology

A simile is a comparison between two things using *like* or *as*.

> **Examples:** Janine is sweet as candy.
>
> Jason is clever like a fox.

A metaphor is a comparison between two things without using *like* or *as*.

> **Examples:** Doreen is my sunshine.
>
> Tony is a bear.

Personification is a figure of speech in which animals, ideas, or inanimate objects are given human characteristics.

> **Examples:** The wind whistled through the trees.
>
> The mirror stared back at me.

Imagery is writing that appeals to the five senses. It's most common form appeals to a reader's sense of sight, using such descriptive language that the reader can "see" the scene in his or her head.

> **Examples:** The garden is full of budding yellow daffodils.
>
> The dog's warm, wet tongue smeared itself all over Filipe's face.

Rhythm is the beat in language that is created by patterns of stressed and unstressed syllables.

> **Example:** To MAR-ket, to MAR-ket, to BUY a fat PIG.

Rhyme is the repetition of sounds at the end of two or more words. In poetry, this often occurs with the last word of a line.

> **Example:** I love my <u>wife</u>,
>
> I love my <u>life</u>.

Alliteration is the repetition of initial consonant sounds in a word.

Examples: Lucky little Lyle

Katie quietly cut the kiwi.

Commonly Confused Words

ACCEPT – verb meaning *to receive*

I **accept** your gift with pleasure.

EXCEPT – preposition meaning *to take or leave out*

Everyone is going to the movies **except** for Marco.

ADVICE – noun meaning *guidance, recommendation*

My mother always gives me good **advice**.

ADVISE – verb meaning *to counsel or inform, to give advice*

She particularly loves to **advise** me on my love life.

AFFECT – verb meaning *to influence*

Sleepiness can severely **affect** your driving ability.

EFFECT – noun meaning *result*

The **effects** of the bad economy are felt in every city in the country.

A LOT – two words meaning *many*

You can tell she has **a lot** of friends because her phone is always ringing.

ALOT – (written as one word) no such word

ALLUSION – noun meaning an *indirect reference*

Anna made an **allusion** to her past when she mentioned the accident.

ILLUSION – noun meaning *a false perception of reality*

The magician seemed to turn a rock into gold, but it was only an **illusion**.

ALL READY – two words meaning *prepared*

The crowd was **all ready** for the soccer game to begin.

ALREADY – adverb meaning *by this time*

The game had **already** begun when we arrived.

ALL RIGHT – two words meaning everything is correct

You can miss a few questions on the quiz, but it's better if you get them **all right**.

ALRIGHT – a non-standard form of *all right* meaning *fine* or *satisfactory*

Everyone was **alright** after the accident, apart from a few scrapes and scratches.

ALTOGETHER – adverb meaning *entirely*

I felt **altogether** frightened by his pale face and dark eyes.

ALL TOGETHER – two words meaning *gathered, with everything in one place*

Please gather your belongings **all together** before we leave.

APART – adverb meaning *separated*

It's hard to keep those two lovebirds **apart** these days.

A PART – two words meaning *to be a section of*

Those two pages are only **a part** of the whole book.

ASCENT – noun meaning *a climb*

The **ascent** up the hill to the cave was a difficult a climb for me.

ASSENT – verb meaning *to agree*

Sick as she was, Shawna refused to **assent** to the treatment.

BREATH – noun meaning *air inhaled or exhaled*

I had a hard time catching my **breath** after that roller coaster ride.

BREATHE – verb meaning *to inhale or exhale*

The air was so smoky, I could hardly **breathe**.

CAPITAL – noun meaning (1) *a seat of government;* (2) *financial resources;* or (3) *upper case letters*

(1) The **capital** of California is Sacramento.
(2) The bank had enough **capital** to continue making loans.
(3) Remember to use a **capital** letter at the beginning of every sentence.

CAPITOL – noun meaning *the actual building in which a legislative body meets*

Meet me on the steps of the **capitol**, and we will go in to meet the senator together.

CITE – verb meaning *to quote or document*

Be careful to **cite** all your sources when writing a research paper.

SIGHT – noun meaning *vision*

At the **sight** of her smile, I knew everything would be fine.

SITE – noun meaning *position or place*

The **site** of the accident was at 23rd Street and Montana Boulevard.

COMPLEMENT – (1) noun meaning *something that completes;* or (2) verb meaning *to complete*

(1) That red scarf is a perfect **complement** to your outfit.
(2) A red scarf would **complement** your outfit beautifully.

COMPLIMENT – (1) noun meaning *praise;* or (2) verb meaning *to praise*

(1) Everyone loves getting **compliments** on a new haircut.
(2) I **complimented** Maria on her new haircut.

CONSCIENCE – noun meaning *sense of right and wrong*

Paulo's **conscience** was bothering him after he ate the pie we were saving for dessert.

CONSCIOUS – noun meaning *awake*

Although he was barely **conscious**, Dipak kept calling for his brother.

COUNCIL – noun meaning *a group that consults or advises*

Mr. Jackson was thinking of running for city **council** in the next election.

COUNSEL – verb meaning *to advise*

My brother was considering buying a motorcycle, but I **counseled** him not to.

ELICIT – verb meaning *to draw or bring out*

It was hard to **elicit** any response from the shy little girl.

ILLICIT – adjective meaning *illegal*

Annika's **illicit** behavior is sure to get her in trouble with the police one day.

ENSURE – verb meaning *to make certain*

Try to **ensure** that you use all the words on this list correctly.

INSURE – verb meaning *to protect against risk*

John can't afford to **insure** his car.

ITS – pronoun meaning *of* or *belonging to it*

Maine is famous for **its** clam chowder.

IT'S – contraction for *it is*

With a fresh paint job, **it's** possible for your car to look brand new.

LEAD – (1) noun meaning *a type of metal;* or (2) verb meaning *to guide*

(1) Thirty years ago, most paint contained dangerous levels of **lead**.
(2) Let me **lead** you through the tunnel together.

LED – past tense of the verb *to lead*

Jacob **led** us to the place where he thought he lost his wallet.

LOSE – verb meaning (1) *to misplace;* or (2) *to not win*

(1) I often **lose** my car keys.
(2) I am probably going to **lose** this argument.

LOOSE – noun meaning *to not be tight*

Since I've lost a little weight, my ring is very **loose** on my finger.

PASSED – verb, past tense of *to pass*, meaning *to have gone by*

We just **passed** the street that we needed to turn right on.

PAST – (1) adjective meaning *belonging to a former time or place;* or (2) noun meaning *a time gone by*

(1) In the **past**, I collected baseball cards, but now I collect beer mugs.
(2) My library book was **past** due.

PRECEDE – verb meaning *to come before*

A throbbing headache often **precedes** a cold.

PROCEED – verb meaning *to go forward*

Proceed to the next available window when your name is called.

PRINCIPAL – (1) adjective meaning *most important;* or (2) noun meaning *a person who has authority*

(1) The **principal** ingredient in chicken soup is, of course, chicken.
(2) The **principal** of the school was fired for stealing lunches.

PRINCIPLE – noun meaning *a general or fundamental truth*

It is important to learn the basic **principles** of cooking before experimenting with fancy recipes.

STATIONARY – adjective meaning *standing still*

Most cars remain **stationary** until you push the gas.

STATIONERY – noun meaning *writing paper*

It's more fun to write letters when you have pretty **stationery**.

THAN – used for making comparisons

Mark would rather play video games **than** watch television.

THEN – meaning *at that time* or *next*

I ran for five miles and **then** stopped to catch my breath.

THEIR – possessive pronoun meaning *belonging to them*

Their kids usually have soccer games on Friday nights.

THERE – indicates location

Let's put our picnic blanket down over **there**.

THEY'RE – contraction meaning *they are*

Before they start work, **they're** going shopping for new clothes.

THROUGH – preposition meaning (1) *by means of;* (2) *finished;* or (3) *into or out of*

(1) It was only **through** hard work that he succeeded.
(2) I'm **through** with arguing about that.
(3) Go **through** the door on the right and you will find what you are looking for.

THREW – verb, past tense of *to throw*

I **threw** those magazines away weeks ago.

THRU – abbreviation for *through;* not appropriate in formal writing

It is quicker to use the drive-**thru** window than to go inside to order your hamburgers.

TO – preposition meaning *toward*

Mia went **to** school at night for three years.

TOO – adverb meaning (1) *also;* or (2) *excessively*

(1) Anna saw a new movie last weekend; Martine did, **too**.
(2) It was **too** cold outside to go swimming.

TWO – a number

I already have **two** dogs, and I still want another one!

WEAR – verb meaning *to be dressed in*

Because I don't look good in green, I never know what to **wear** on St. Patrick's Day.

WHERE – (1) noun or (2) adverb meaning *place* or *location*

(1) **Where** do you want to go for dinner?
(2) That is **where** the fatal accident happened last year.

WHOSE – possessive form of *who,* meaning *belonging to*

Whose socks are these that I found under the bed?

WHO'S – contraction meaning *who is*

Who's going to the game on Saturday night?

YOUR – possessive adjective meaning *belonging to you*

Your paycheck is going to have a little extra bonus added to it this month.

YOU'RE – contraction meaning *you are*

You're not going to make it to work on time if you keep hitting the snooze button.

MLA Guidelines

Use the following guidelines to help you format your paper and cite your sources.

Formatting Your Paper

- Use a standard, easily readable typeface like Times New Roman and a 12-point font.
- Double-space, and margins should be 1 inch on all sides.
- Indent the first word of each paragraph. Do not skip extra lines between paragraphs.
- Number the pages of your essay. Do not include a separate title page.
- Include a Works Cited page at the end of your paper.

Citations Within Your Paper

You must give credit for all information you include in your writing that comes from another source, whether it is quoted directly or paraphrased. If your information or quote comes from a source that has an author and page number, you must provide this information within the text of your paper. If the author's name is included in the sentence, you do not need to repeat the name. Notice that the period at the end of the sentence goes *after* the citation.

Quotation: "Fifty-seven percent of all adults exhibit the recessive trait," (Holloway 23).

Paraphrase: According to the research most adults are likely to suffer from this disease late in life (Holloway 23).

Quotation: Dr. Holloway has found that, "Fifty-seven percent of all adults exhibit the recessive trait" (23).

Paraphrase: According to research by Dr. James Holloway, most adults are likely to suffer from this disease late in life (23).

When a source has two or three authors, include all last names. When a source has more than three authors, use (Crosetto et al. 36). *Et al* means "and others."

For a source with no listed author—for example, a Web site, newspaper article, or encyclopedia entry—use the title of the article if it is short or an abbreviated version if the title is very long.

Example: The repeated use of tanning salons can cause skin cancer ("The Dangers of Going Brown" 68).

To cite information from a personal interview you conducted, include the last name of the person you interviewed.

Example: "I deeply regret having maintained a deep tan all my life" (Schneider).

To cite information from an electronic source that includes an author and page number, use the same format you would use for a print source. If no page information is available, simply cite the author's name within parenthesis. If you are citing from an electronic source that does not include an author's name, put the title of the Web page or article in quotation marks within parenthesis.

Example of electronic source with author but no page number: Fair-skinned individuals are more prone to be susceptible to skin cancer (Connor).

Example of electronic source with no author: Many moisturizing lotions now include sunscreen ("Saving Your Skin").

Works Cited Page

Papers written in MLA documentation style should include a Works Cited page as a last page. The page will list every source you cite in the essay. Use the following guidelines to create your Works Cited page:

- Title the page "Works Cited."
- List sources in alphabetical order by the authors' last names. If no authors are listed, use the source title.
- Double-space the list.
- If you don't have an author's name, begin the entry with the main word of the article or book title (ignore *A, An,* or *The* when alphabetizing).
- Underline the title of books, magazines, or journals.
- Put the title of articles inside quotation marks.
- The first line of the entry should be flush with the left margin, and the subsequent lines indented 5 spaces to the right.
- Abbreviate the names of all months except *May*, *June*, and *July*.

Examples
Books

Author's last name, First name. "Article Title." <u>Book Title</u>. City: Publisher, date.

Book with One Author

Rosen, Howard. "The Effects of Exposure." <u>Skin Care Today, Tomorrow, and Forever</u>. New York: Pocket Books, 2008.

Book with More than One Author

Brown, Martha and Jorge Martin. <u>Global Warming: What You Need to Know</u>. Portsmouth: Vantage, 2007.

Books with No Author

<u>The Guide to Tanning Techniques</u>. New York: Starlight Books, 2008.

Articles with Authors

Author's last name, First name. "Article." <u>Title of Publication</u> Issue/Volume #. Date of Publication: page(s).

Magazine Article

Allen, Emily. "Who Needs the Sun?" <u>Beauty News</u> Dec. 2008: 27.

Newspaper Article

Greer, Michael. "Running on Empty." <u>Los Angeles Times</u> 14 Mar. 2009: A5, col. 1.

Journal Article

With journals be sure to include volume and issue numbers along with the date and page numbers.

Williams, Thomas. "Research into Sunshine." <u>Journal of Health</u> vol. 12/4. May 2008: 22–26.

Articles without Authors

If an article has no author listed, begin the entry with the title.

Magazine Article with No Author

"Everything Under the Sun." <u>Healthy Living</u> Dec. 2008: 32–36.

Newspaper Article with No Author

"Pale Is Beautiful." <u>The Washington Post</u> 25 Aug. 2009: A5.

Encyclopedia Article with No Author

"Melanoma." <u>Encyclopedia Britannica</u> 2002 ed.

Reference Books

Author last name, First name (if given). "Article Title." <u>Title of Book</u>. City of Publication: Publisher, Year.

When citing familiar reference books, full publication information is not necessary. Give the edition (if available) and the year of publication. If articles are arranged alphabetically, volume and page numbers are not necessary.

Daniels, Leo. "Rivers." <u>The World Book Encyclopedia</u>. 2006.

When citing less familiar reference books, give full publication information. Give the number of volumes for multi-volume sets.

Forrest, Josephine. "Weather Patterns." <u>Encyclopedia of Weather</u>. Ed. Robert Daley. 2nd ed. 4 vols. New York: Macmillan, 2007.

Electronic Sources

When citing from an online source, include all the information you would include for print sources that is available. Include the author (if available), the title of the individual page or article you are citing, the name of the Web site, the date the page/article was created or last updated, the date you found the information, and the entire Web site address.

Author's last name, First name. "Article Title." <u>Name of Site</u>. Date of publication/revision.
   Retrieval date <Web address>.

Online Newspaper Article

Thompson. Edward. "Doctors Don't Agree." <u>New York Times</u>. 23 Feb. 2008. 25 Oct. 2009
   <http://www.newyorktimes.com/EThompson/2-23-08/04I-068-idx.hmtl>.

Online Article/Source with No Author

"Save Your Skin." <u>Harpers Online</u>. 20 June 2007. 2 Oct. 2008
   <http://www.harpers.com/archives/issue/062008/sys.html>.

Interviews

Subject's last name, First name. Type of Interview. Date of interview.

Email Interview

Schneider, Erin. E-mail interview. 18 Feb. 2009.

Face-to-Face or Phone Interview

Schneider, Erin. TTY interview. 18 Feb. 2009.

Common Editing Marks

Symbol	Explanation	Example	Corrected Example
≡	**Capitalize letter**	Mandy starts school in september.	Mandy starts school in September.
/	**Use lower case**	I want my Mother to see this movie.	I want my mother to see this movie.
∧	**Insert word**	Jeffrey is a young man. *troubled*	Jeffrey is a troubled young man.
∧	**Insert comma**	My car a real beauty, is my pride and joy.	My car, a real beauty, is my pride and joy.
?	**Insert question mark**	Where are you going with that soup?	Where are you going with that soup?
⊙	**Insert period**	I'm leaving for the mall right now Do you want to come with me?	I'm leaving for the mall right now. Do you want to come with me?
ℊ	**Delete**	Jared called up me on his cell phone.	Jared called me on his cell phone.
⬭ or *sp*	**Spelling error**	I still have not recieved a response from the gas company.	I still have not received a response from the gas company.
¶	**Insert new paragraph**	The second point I want to make . . .	The second point I want to make . . .
∼	**Transpose letters or words**	Jacob relies mostly on his sister for advice.	Jacob mostly relies on his sister for advice.

Glossary

······················· **A** ·······················

academic writing   writing that fulfills a purpose of education in a college or university. For most teachers, the term implies student writing in response to an academic assignment, or the writing that trained "academics" (teachers and researchers) do for their professional lives. Academic writing usually presents information or an argument.

active voice   one of the two "voices" of verbs. When the verb of a sentence is in the active voice, the subject does the acting.
   Example: The pitcher <u>threw</u> the ball. (*Threw* is in the active voice because *pitcher* is the subject, and the pitcher does the throwing.) Contrast with *passive voice*.

alliteration   the repetition of beginning consonant sounds
   Example: <u>S</u>amuel <u>s</u>aid <u>s</u>omething <u>s</u>illy.

analytical   requiring analysis, the separating of a whole into its elements or basic parts and explaining them

analyze   to break something down into its basic parts and explain them

anecdote   a short account of an interesting or humorous incident

antecedent   the particular noun or phrase that a pronoun is substituting for or refers to
   Example: After <u>Lorenzo</u> ate, <u>he</u> went for a walk. (*Lorenzo* is the antecedent of *he*.)

appositive   a word or phrase that explains or gives more information about a noun or pronoun
   Example: Sara, <u>the night clerk</u>, had to leave early. (*the night clerk* is an appositive that gives more information about the noun *Sara*.)

argue   to present reasons or facts in order to persuade someone to do something or believe a certain way

argument   reasons and facts that a writer uses to persuade readers

audience   the intended readers of a piece of writing

autobiographical incident   an event that happened to someone, told by that person

······················· **B** ·······················

bias   a partiality or leaning of the mind that prevents impartial thinking or judgment

biographical information   information about a person's life

block method   an organization pattern for a comparison/contrast essay (also known as the whole-versus-whole pattern or the consecutive pattern). In this pattern, the writer discusses each subject or topic separately. Contrast with *point method*.

body   the middle paragraphs of an essay, which develop and support the thesis

brainstorm   to gather ideas by writing down all the thoughts that come to mind without judging them

······················· **C** ·······················

call to action   a suggestion that asks a reader to think or act in a certain way. A call to action is usually part of an essay's conclusion.

cause-and-effect essay an essay that explains why or how some event happened, and what resulted from the event. This kind of essay can explain both causes and effects, or it can address one or the other. A cause essay usually explains the reasons why something happened. An effect essay discusses what happens after a specific event or circumstance.

chronological order the order in which events happen; time order

cite to give information about the source of quoted material or ideas

clarity clearness of thought or expression

clause a group of words containing a subject and a verb. See *dependent clause, independent clause*.

cluster a kind of graphic organizer for grouping similar things

cohesive all the parts fit together to create a logical, united whole

comma splice an error in which two independent clauses (sentences) are separated only by a comma
    Example: High heels can be dangerous, they can cause back problems.

commentary written explanation or remarks

compare to explain how two or more things are alike

comparison/contrast essay an essay that compares, contrasts, or does both

complex sentence a sentence made of one independent clause and one or more dependent clauses
    Example: We will eat at home if the restaurant is closed.

compound sentence a sentence made of two or more independent clauses joined with a comma and coordinating conjunction or with a semicolon
    Example: We traveled by boat, and we had a wonderful time.

compound-complex sentence a sentence made of two or more independent clauses and at least one dependent clause
    Example: Lightning flashed and rain fell as we drove through the night.

concession the acknowledging of something as being true, just, or proper and then overcoming it with logic or a solution

concise using few words to say much

conclusion the end of a piece of writing that restates the thesis, gives the writing a sense of completeness, and leaves a final impression on the reader

contrast to explain how two or more things are different

coordinating conjunction a connecting word that connects equal elements, such as the independent clauses in a compound sentence. *For, and, nor, but, or, yet,* and *so* are the coordinating conjunctions.
    Example: She worked hard, <u>and</u> her performance improved.

counter-argument an argument that opposes a thesis or point

credibility the quality of being believable or trustworthy

criteria standards, rules, or tests on which a judgment or decision can be based

critique to examine both the positive and negative aspects of an issue or topic

D

dependent clause a clause that cannot stand alone as a sentence because it is not a complete thought
    Example: because it guides readers through the essay

describe to write about a subject so the reader can easily visualize it; to tell how something looks or happens, including how, who, where, and why

details less important facts or ideas that give more information about a topic

development the support given to a main idea by details, examples, facts, anecdotes, arguments, etc.

discuss to examine or consider in detail; to give a complete and detailed description and explanation, including supporting information, examples, points for and against, and then evaluate

draft a preliminary version of a written work; to create by thinking and writing

E

edit to make changes to a text, correcting errors

elaboration description, explanation, examples, and other details that thoroughly develop a point or basic idea

elements of literature figurative language, imagery, sound devices, plot, and other aspects of literature that help convey meaning and produce effects in readers

essay a piece of writing several paragraphs or longer that explains the writer's view on a topic

evaluate to examine and judge the importance, worth, or quality of something

evidence knowledge on which to base belief; something that provides or tends to provide proof

expository writing a type of writing used to explain, describe, give information, or inform

F

figurative language a way of describing an ordinary thing in an unordinary way; language that describes one thing by comparing it to something very different

fragment a group of words that do not express a complete thought; an incomplete sentence

G

graphic organizer a visual way of organizing ideas and analyzing relationships. Graphic organizers help people convert and compress seemingly unconnected information into structured simple-to-understand "pictures."

I

illustrate to clarify by using examples or comparisons

imagery the representation of sensory experiences (sight, touch, smell, hearing, taste) in language

inciting incident the event that starts or brings about the main conflict in a story

independent clause a clause that can stand alone as a sentence because it is a complete thought
    Example: Isabella is a manager.

inference a conclusion made by combining what is in the text with prior knowledge or experience

interpret to give or provide the meaning of; explain

interpretation an explanation of the meaning or importance of something

introduction the beginning of an essay, which introduces the topic and draws the reader in

L

logic sound reasoning, which can be be supported, justified, or defended

M

metaphor a figure of speech in which two things are compared without using the words *like* or *as*
Example: I wanted to run, but my legs were rubber.

mood the feeling that a literary work conveys to readers. Mood is created through the use of plot, character, the author's descriptions, etc.

N

narration a telling of events, especially in chronological order; a story

O

organization the arrangement of ideas in a piece of writing

outline a list of ideas in which numbers and letters are used to show how the ideas are related to each other

P

paragraph a group of sentences that usually develops one idea

paraphrase a restatement of another person's writing in your own words

passive voice one of the two "voices" of verbs. In passive voice, the subject of the sentence does not do any of the acting; it is acted upon. For example, in "The ball was thrown by the pitcher," the ball (the subject) doesn't do anything. It is acted upon (thrown). Contrast with *active voice*.

personal pronoun a pronoun that refers to a specific person, place, or thing. The personal pronouns are *I, me, myself, we, us, ourselves, you, yourself, yourselves, he, him, himself, she, her, herself, it, itself, they, them, themselves.*

personification a figure of speech in which an animal or inanimate object is given human qualities
Example: The ship began to creak and protest as it struggled against the rising sea.

persuade to cause someone to believe or act in a certain way. Writers persuade by using logical appeals (arguments giving reasons supported by sound evidence); emotional appeals (arguments that target the reader's feelings); and ethical appeals (arguments that reach out to the reader's sense of right and wrong)

persuasive writing writing done for the purpose of persuading an audience

plagiarism presenting the words or ideas of others as though they were your own

point of view belief, opinion, or attitude

point method an organizational pattern for a comparison/contrast essay (also known as the point-by-point method or the simultaneous method). The writer discusses each subject or topic at the same time. Contrast with *block method*.

prompt a set of directions for a writing assignment

pronoun   a word that replaces either a noun or another pronoun. There are several different kinds of pronouns.

    Example: Angela borrowed several hammers, and <u>she</u> (replaces the noun *Angela*) will return <u>them</u> (replaces the plural noun *hammers*) tomorrow.

proofread   to reread a text to find and correct errors

purpose   the reason for writing. Writers typically write to inform, to persuade, to express, or to entertain.

························· **Q** ·························

question paper   a list of things a reader finds puzzling in a piece of writing

quotation   exact words of another person that are repeated or copied

························· **R** ·························

redundancy   unnecessary repetition

reference   a work used as a source in another piece of writing; a short note recognizing a source of information or of a quoted passage

reflective writing   autobiographical writing that presents an incident, analyzes or interprets it, and then explains its significance

reflexive pronouns   pronouns such as *myself, yourself,* and *ourselves* that rename subjects of action verbs

    Example: Mr. Ota poured <u>himself</u> a cup of coffee. (*Himself* renames *Mr. Ota,* which is the subject of the verb *poured.*)

refute   to disprove by argument, evidence, or proof

research   a search for knowledge; a systematic investigation to establish facts

respond   to state your overall reaction to the subject, then support your opinion with reasons and examples

revise   to change writing in order to improve or correct it

rhetorical question   a figure of speech in the form of a question that is asked for persuasive effect. No reply is expected. A rhetorical question encourages readers to think about the implied answer to the question.

    Example: How much longer must our people endure this injustice?

rhyme   one of the musical devices in poetry. Rhyme is the repetition of the final stressed vowel and all following sounds in two or more words, (as in <u>sight</u> and <u>flight</u>). Poems can have end rhyme, in which words at the ends of lines rhyme; this is what we usually mean when we say a poem "rhymes."

rhythm   the recurring pattern of stressed (accented, or long) and unstressed (unaccented, or short) syllables in lines of a set length; also known as *meter*

    Example: Notice the pattern of unaccented and accented syllables in this line of poetry: Was THIS / the FACE / that LAUNCHED / a THOU /sand SHIPS?

rubric   a scoring tool that lists the levels of quality for a piece of writing, along with the criteria for each level

run-on sentence   two or more independent clauses joined as one sentence without proper punctuation or connecting words

    Example: In time I hope to finish college I will then look for a better job.

S

sensory detail language that describes how something looks, feels, smells, sounds, or tastes

sentence combining the process of combining the short sentences in choppy writing to produce a longer, more sophisticated sentence

sentence structure (syntax) the sequence in which words are put together to form sentences

setting the time and place during which a story takes place

simile a figure of speech in which the comparison includes *like* or *as*
> **Example:** The woman ran from the house like some huge awkward chicken torn, squawking, from its coop.

simple sentence a sentence containing one independent clause

sound device any of the techniques that poets use to enhance the auditory appeal of poetry. *Alliteration* and *rhyme* are two examples of sound devices.

source a work from which you paraphrase, summarize, or quote

statistics numerical facts or data

style the characteristics of a writer's work, such as word choice, sentence structure, level of formality, and the attitude toward subject matter

subject the sentence part that tells who or what the sentence is about

subordinating conjunction a conjunction that appears at the beginning of a dependent clause to connect it to an independent clause
> **Example:** I will go to the party <u>even though</u> I may have to leave early.

summary a brief statement of the main ideas and important details in a piece of writing

supporting points ideas that support the thesis of an essay. The supporting points comprise the body of the essay

T

template a predesigned, customized format and structure, as for a fax, letter, or expense report, ready to be filled in

thesis, thesis statement the main point or controlling idea of an essay

tone a writer's attitude towards his or her subject

topic sentence the sentence that tells the main idea of a paragraph

transition the connection (a word, phrase, clause, sentence, or even an entire paragraph) between two parts of a piece of writing that contributes to coherence. Transitions are accomplished mainly through pronouns, repetition of key words, and specific transition words.

transition words and phrases words or groups of words that signals the way ideas are related
> **Examples:** *in addition, however, finally, therefore, in other words*

U

usage the customary manner in which a language (or a form of a language) is spoken or written

V

Venn diagram   a diagram that uses overlapping circles to compare and contrast information

verb   the part of a sentence that tells what the subject is or does

voice   the writer's style as demonstrated through word choice and sentence structure

W

working thesis statement   a placeholder thesis statement

works cited page   a page listing the sources quoted, summarized, or paraphrased in an essay

writing on demand   writing produced in response to a prompt, usually within a time limit

Index